IN THE LAND OF THE INCAS

Evening Calm, Lake Titicaca

IN THE
LAND *of the* INCAS

by
F. A. STAHL

"How beautiful upon the mountains are the feet of him that bringeth good tidings, that publisheth peace; that bringeth good tidings of good, that publisheth salvation; that saith unto Zion, Thy God reigneth!" Isaiah 52:7.

*I*n honor, memory, and recognition of the great missionaries Fernando and Ana Stahl, Donald J. Chavez—a layman—has asked, ordered, and sponsored the reprint and publication of the book, **In the Land of the Incas**, by Fernando Stahl.

These self-supporting missionaries, Fernando and Ana Stahl, together with their son Wallace and wife Graciela, arrived with the help of God at Peru, So. America. Despite the opposition, hate, and persecution led by the leaders of the popular church and its followers (priests, landowners, judges, and some authorities of the land), who kept the numerically dominant indigenous (descendants of the Incas) in ignorance, superstition, and at bay. Nevertheless, the Stahls, with the power of the Gospel, continued their arduous work for almost 30 years (1909–1938), until their mission was accomplished. They, in the name of Jesus Christ, SET THE CAPTIVES FREE, for the honor and glory of God, the Almighty creator of the universe.
—Donald J. Chavez

TEACH Services, Inc.
PUBLISHING
www.TEACHServices.com • (800) 367-1844

World rights reserved. This book or any portion thereof may not be copied or reproduced in any form or manner whatever, except as provided by law, without the written permission of the publisher, except by a reviewer
who may quote brief passages in a review.

The author assumes full responsibility for the accuracy of all facts and quotations as cited in this book. The opinions expressed in this book are the author's personal views and interpretations, and do not necessarily
reflect those of the publisher.

This book is provided with the understanding that the publisher is not engaged in giving spiritual, legal, medical, or other professional advice.
If authoritative advice is needed, the reader should seek the counsel
of a competent professional.

Facsimile Reproduction
As this book played a formative role in the development of Christian thought and the publisher feels that this book, with its candor and depth, still holds significance for the church today. Therefore the publisher has chosen to reproduce this historical classic from an original copy. Frequent variations in the quality of the print are unavoidable due to the condition of the original. Thus the print may look darker or lighter or appear to be missing detail,
more in some places than in others.

Copyright © 2006 TEACH Services, Inc.
ISBN-13: 978-1-57258-454-9 (Paperback)
Library of Congress Control Number: 2006930558

TEACH Services, Inc.
P U B L I S H I N G
www.TEACHServices.com • (800) 367-1844

To those who desire to see this gospel of the kingdom go to all nations in this generation this book is dedicated. May it be an inspiration to all to make great sacrifices for those who know not Christ.

Preface

"Half the world knows not how the other half lives." We are likely to become so wrapped up in our pleasures, ambitions, and even sorrows, as to forget the needs of the great world outside, and fail to consider that we are at least in some degree responsible for the condition of the human family as a whole.

It is my purpose to show that many who are living in idolatry, wretchedness, and degradation, and who have customs which we do not like, are in this condition because of ignorance of the truth, and that when they learn "the better way," they develop into noble characters. It is true that some do not take advantage of opportunity when it comes to them; nevertheless, let the opportunity be given them.

Our Lord says, "This gospel of the kingdom shall be preached in all the world for a witness;" not that all will accept it, but that all may have the privilege. When we share our blessings, we find them greater, and our sorrows lighter; and if we aspire to real greatness, the words of our Saviour found in Mark 10: 43, 44 will help us to attain that greatness which will always endure.

I desire to express my gratitude to the officers of the General Conference, from whom I have always received the kindest and most courteous help. If my work for the Indians can be called a success, that success is in large measure attributable to encouragement from these brethren.

My acknowledgments are also due to Mr. F. E. Hinckley, superintendent of the Harvard Observatory at Arequipa, Peru, who, when I was worn with work, opened his hospitable home to me, and who gave me instruction in photography, and furnished some of the photographs used in illustrating this book; to Elder M. C. Wilcox and Mrs. Adelaide D. Wellman for many valuable suggestions and for correcting the manuscript; to all connected with the Pacific Press Publishing Association, who were very friendly and obliging during my stay at that institution; and to Professor M. E. Kern, whose kind persistence is directly responsible for my undertaking this work at this time.

F. A. STAHL.

CONTENTS

CHAPTER		PAGE
	Introduction	17
I	On the Roof of the World	35
II	Inca Ruins and Traditions	49
III	A Primitive People	68
IV	Missionary Mining	87
V	Exigencies of Missionary Pioneering	98
VI	An Oppressed Race	105
VII	A Transformation	126
VIII	By Way of Encouragement	144
IX	"Christianity" That Is Not Christian	157
X	Help from High Sources	183
XI	Reconnoitering	188
XII	Proof of Appreciation	202
XIII	The Broken Pebble	220
XIV	A Mysterious Rescue	233
XV	Enemies Disarmed	253
XVI	The Quichuas Calling for Help	261
XVII	In Perils Oft	272
XVIII	Supplementary Notes	286
XIX	Among the Missions About Lake Titicaca	295

(11)

ILLUSTRATIONS

EVENING CALM - - - - - - - *Frontispiece*	
MAP OF THE LAKE TITICACA REGION - - - -	16
TRANSVERSE SECTIONS OF THE ANDES - - - -	19
MONOLITHIC IMAGE AT TIAHUANUCO - - - -	21
PART OF THE ORIGINAL WALL, TEMPLE OF THE SUN, CUZCO - - - - - - - - - - -	25
STREET IN CUZCO SHOWING ORIGINAL INCA WALLS -	27
ANCIENT INCA MASONRY CONTRASTED WITH INFERIOR MODERN CONSTRUCTION - - - - - -	29
F. A. STAHL, THE AUTHOR - - - - - - -	24
LANDING PLACE, MOLLENDO, "THE ROUGHEST PORT IN THE WORLD" - - - - - - - -	36
THE FAMOUS SAND DUNES BETWEEN MOLLENDO AND AREQUIPA - - - - - - - - - -	38
STREET MARKET, AREQUIPA, PERU, SHOWING THE FRUIT OF SOIL AND LOOM - - - - -	40
MOUNT MISTI, A LIVE VOLCANO, AREQUIPA, PERU -	45
"LA BALSA" (STRAW BOAT), LAKE TITICACA - -	47
AN ARCHWAY IN CUZCO - - - - - - -	50
A WALL OF CORICANCHA, JOINTS IN MASONRY ALMOST INVISIBLE - - - - - - - - -	52
INDIAN WOMAN WEAVING PONCHOS - - - - -	55
HARVESTING THE WOOL CROP FROM ALPACAS - -	57
A CHOLO WOMAN AND CHILD - - - - - -	61
A MOUNTAIN COACH - - - - - - -	65
INDIANS OF SOUTH AMERICA - - - - - -	69
AN ORDINARY PERUVIAN ROAD - - - - - -	73
INDIAN OF THE TROPICS OF THE YUNGAS OF BOLIVIA -	77
A NATURAL CUT - - - - - - - -	81
A CHILD OF PERU - - - - - - - -	86
ALTAR ON THE SUMMIT OF ONE OF THE HIGHEST MOUNTAINS - - - - - - - - -	91
MISSIONARIES GREETED WITH FLAGS BY THE QUENUANI SCHOOL - - - - - - - - - -	95
STREET SCENE IN LA PAZ - - - - - -	99
A PERUVIAN MOUNTAINEER - - - - - - -	103
INDIAN WOMAN GRINDING BARLEY - - - -	106
A "FINCA" (FARM) IN THE CUZCO VALLEY - - -	111
LLAMAS CARRYING GRAIN OVER THE MOUNTAINS -	119
A MASK USED BY INDIAN DANCERS - - - - -	121
TEACHING CHILDREN TO DANCE AND DRINK ALCOHOL	123
THE FIRST MISSION HEADQUARTERS - - - -	127
INDIAN WATER CARRIER - - - - - - -	133
INDIAN 110 YEARS OLD, FROM WHOM THE FIRST MISSION LAND WAS PURCHASED - - - - -	135
AYMARA INDIAN HAIR DRESSING - - - - -	139

(13)

ILLUSTRATIONS

Indian Convert Plowing with a Crooked Stick	141
The Sick Coming to the Plateria Dispensary	144
Our First Mission House Going Up at Plateria	147
Our First Choir Among the Indians	151
A Group of Straw Boats on Lake Titicaca	153
Dariteo, One of Our Indian Teachers	159
Indians and Shrine Before a Church Near Cuzco	165
The First Baptism Among the Indians	169
Indian Families Returning from Market, Puno, Peru	173
Catholic Church at Laraos Where Meetings Were Held by Our Missionaries	177
Mrs. Stahl and Her Indian School	187
Chulpa, or Royal Monument, Umayo, Peru	189
Meeting with the Indians—Always the Best of Attention	195
Indians Making Grass Boats	199
After the Sabbath Services at Plateria	203
Chief Camacho and Juan Huanca	207
Inca Ruins, South America	209
Lunch Time	213
Family Group of Indians Near Lake Titicaca	221
Indian Officials, Called "Hilacatas"	223
As the Indians Often Meet Our Missionaries	227
Mr. and Mrs. Stahl About to Start for a Visit Among the Indians	235
High Mountain Indians	243
The Island of the Sun, Lake Titicaca	249
Our Second Mission Station	255
Communion Services Among the Indians	260
The First Messengers from the Quichuas	262
Among the Indians of the High Mountain Region, Elevation 16,000 Feet	265
"Treasures of Snow and Hail"	267
Indian Teachers Now in the Field	269
Luciano, Our First Indian Pastor, and His Wife	278
Honorato, Rescued by the Gospel from Deplorable Darkness, and Now a Teacher	279
Peruvian Women	283
Lake Titicaca Colporteurs' Institute Held in 1919	287
The Main Station as It Now Is	293
Baptism in Lake Titicaca	297
A Road Along the Edge of a Two Thousand Foot Precipice	299

*G*OD commendeth His love toward us, in that, while we were yet sinners, Christ died for us. Romans 5:8.

MAP OF THE LAKE TITICACA REGION

Introduction

[Note.—The facts of this "Introduction," it is perhaps needless to say, have been gathered largely from Prescott's great work, "Peru." Other more recent works, as "Peru," by Geraldine Guinness, "South of Panama," by Dr. Edward Alsworth Ross, of Wisconsin University, and articles in magazines, notably in the *National Geographic,* have been consulted. We make special note of the issues of April, 1913, February, 1915, and May, 1916, containing reports of the explorations of the National Geographic Society and Yale University, by Hiram Bingham, director. The author of the story which follows, Mr. F. A. Stahl, has been too busy in his medical missionary work to give attention to this historical sketch. Yet the publishers have thought that such a sketch is needed to give the proper setting to the heart-gripping story which follows.]

THE COMING OF THE SPANIARDS

IN 1532 and 1533, the Spaniards, led by Francisco Pizarro and Diego de Almagro, both of them without legitimate parentage, without education sufficient to sign their names,— two things not uncommon in the middle ages,— both soldiers of fortune, lured by the greed of gold, entered, under the guise of friendship, into the great empire of the Incas, entrapped and slew the king, Atahualpa, and seized the empire for Spain. Pizarro promised Atahualpa, whom he captured by falsehood and horrible slaughter of his defenseless retinue, his freedom if he would fill a room with gold,—3,366 cubic feet. When the room was nearly filled, Pizarro absolved him from further obligation, trumped up false charges against him, found him guilty of death, and sentenced him to be burned publicly. This was changed to the garrote — choking to death — if Atahualpa would embrace the cross. This he did, and his murderers mourned him as a Christian. Treachery and cruelty marked their every step. Professing to be heralds of the Saviour and Lifegiver, they spread death and desolation everywhere their horses' feet trod or their sabers clanked.

It was a fateful time for the Incas. Their empire spread from and included Ecuador on the north to Argentina on the south, along the mighty backbone of the Andes from Chimborazo to Aconcagua; from the Pacific Ocean on the west into the valley of the Amazon in the east; lying largely in the torrid zone, yet, on account of its high mountains, embracing every variety of soil and climate, from its stretches of burning, shifting sand by the sea to the table-lands 14,000 feet high among the mountains, which, with their everlasting diadems of snow, tower into the heavens to a height of 20,000 feet. It was an empire worthy of a great people. But when the Spaniards entered, it was divided through the folly of the last great Inca, Huayna

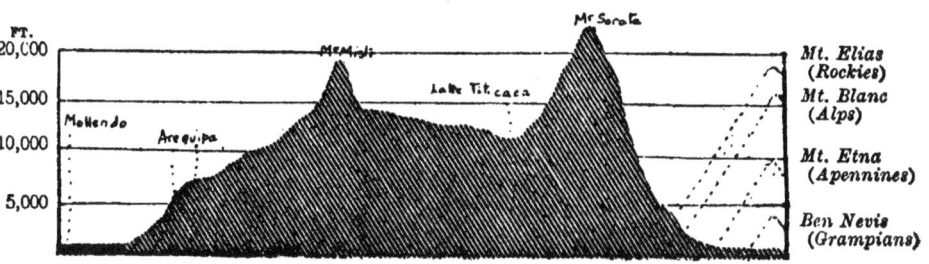

TRANSVERSE SECTIONS OF THE ANDES

Capac, who had broken one of the primal laws of his realm, and given part of the empire, Ecuador, to one who was not a legal heir. Hence division. Hence war. Hence weakness. Otherwise the story might have been different.

WHAT THE SPANIARD FOUND

He found more than savage nomadic tribes living in caves or tents and by the chase. He found more than a wild, barbaric kingdom. He found a civilization, ruled by those whose tradition taught them they were children of the sun. From these children of the sun must the ruler always come pure bred. There were traditions and ruins of a pre-Inca people, who worshiped Pachacamac, the giver and source of life, and built him a mighty temple near where Lima now stands, and represented him by an ugly idol; and perhaps these people were the authors of the monolithic ruins at Tiahuanuco. No one knows. Suffice to say, the Incas in a general way recognized Pachacamac, but their god was Inti, the sun; his consort, the moon; his royal page, Chasca (Venus); the stars, the moon's attendants; the gods of thunder and lightning, the sun's dread ministers; and the rainbow, a revelation of his glory.

The Spaniard found a numerous priesthood, and elaborate sacrifices, ceremonies, and ritual. Human sacrifices were rare. The Inca, or king, was himself divine, far above his people, yet bound to them by the kindness, the fatherhood, the justness of his reign, and their unquestioned reverence for him. They had traditions of the deluge, and a belief in the resurrection, therefore the embalming of their dead.

MONOLITHIC IMAGE AT TIAHUANUCO

The Spaniard found a regular system of education, although no alphabet or hieroglyphics. The *quipu,* an arrangement of colored and knotted cords and threads, was made to do wonderful service in a large number of ways. By it the census was taken yearly and recorded. Account was kept of the amounts of gold and silver in the storehouses. The number of the army, its rank and file, were registered. It served as a memory jogger to the teachers who instructed their students in the history and resources of the empire and the great deeds of the Incas. Its use was a science in itself.

The Spaniard found a very acceptable language in the Quichua, the legal language of the Inca empire, in which the great men and the nobility and the priests were carefully taught, though Aymara and other dialects were spoken among the various peoples composing the empire. Poetry, drama, history, and religion were taught in song and story by word of mouth, and often repeated.

The Spaniard found a system of government that furnished employment for every man, woman, and child in the empire, and provided plentifully for the sick, the infirm, the incapacitated. He found that crops, land, and clothing were so conserved, stored, and divided that no one was in want. He found that the work most detrimental of all to health — mining — was so regulated that none suffered hardship. The laws were few, and penalties severe. Blasphemy against the sun, the cursing of the king, murder, theft, and adultery were punished with death. Arson, removing landmarks, and turning a neighbor's water into one's own plat of land, were severely punished. There were lower courts and higher courts to adjust matters. Everything essential to public order was carefully guarded. The whole empire was divided into groups of ten thousand, one thousand, five hundred, one hundred, fifty, and ten; and over each division, proper officers held to strict account.

The Spaniard found as fine buildings, with the exception of the thatched roofs, as Europe could boast; walls built of tremendous stones, often moved great distances, sometimes so nicely fitted together, even in irregular angles, that it was in some cases well-nigh impossible to distinguish the seam; and these buildings were embellished with such richness of gold, silver, and precious stones as greedy eyes had never seen before. This gold and silver was the largess of the god and goddess of the realm. Gold, their poets sang, was "the tears wept by the sun."

He found marriage regulations wise and strong — polygamy, it is true, among the higher classes; the lower, monogamists. Every family had its land and home, with additional land as children came.

The Spaniard found a military system equal to those of Europe, but without firearms or cavalry. Wars of conquest were continually fought, but manifesting toward the conquered a mercy that barbaric civilizations in Europe never knew.

The Spaniard found a system for raising revenues in which there were neither cruel executions nor oppression nor enslavement. The produce came from the land, the mines, the fisheries. First of all came the tilling of the lands of the sun, then for the needy and ill and infirm, then for the common people, and last for the royal family.

The Spaniard found throughout the empire a system of highways in which the engineering difficulties overcome were worthy of

Part of the Original Wall. Temple of the Sun. Cuzco

a Goethals. Mighty chasms were spanned, deep crevices walled, mountains tunneled, passageways cut through solid rock, drifting sands overcome, morasses bridged; and some of these great roads, despite the corroding influence of the conquerors, still exist.

The Spaniard found a truly scientific system of husbandry, much of which this scientific generation cannot or has not improved upon. The mountain sides were terraced, fertilized, and irrigated. The barren was made to produce. Every available foot of land was used to help in supplying the large population of the empire. The superfluous crops were stored in great stone granaries; and over the splendid roads, the llama bore supplies to those parts of the empire where the people might be in need. Guano was brought from the islands of the coast, and the sea fowls themselves were protected. The wild flocks of alpacas and vicuñas were shielded by law, and quadrennially rounded up, that wool might be obtained from all, and flesh from the males. The domestic flocks of llamas and sheep were systematically moved from place to place to secure sufficient pasturage.

STREET IN CUZCO SHOWING ORIGINAL INCA WALLS

The Spaniard found in the kingdom of the Inca mighty cities and marvelous temples, as Cuzco, a long time the capital of the empire, with its marvelous wealth of gold and silver plate, its gold effigies of the Incas, its gold friezes and cornices of the temple of the sun; as Manchu Picchu, thought to be the "lost city of the Incas," also known as "Tampu-Tocco," or "Window Tavern," the magnificent ruins of which were recently explored by the National Geographic Society and Yale University; and other cities and towns of lesser note that were robbed and ruined by the conquerors.

Into this kingdom of primitive patriarchal despotism — better of its kind than any Europe ever knew — came the Spaniard. He found there, to sum up, no one in want, no beggars or mendicant friars; no lack of life's necessities; the infant, the sick, and the infirm looked after first, not as charity, but as a matter of proper administration; little if any crime or outbreaking immorality; commendable industry, unswerving loyalty to the government; he found art, beauty, skill, greatness.

ANCIENT INCA MASONRY CONTRASTED WITH INFERIOR MODERN CONSTRUCTION

He came in the name of Christ, with fair promise and seeming friendliness. But he came also with a greed of gold that outweighed all love for souls for whom Christ died; came with fanatical unreason, believing that the faith of Christ could be propagated by force, by sword and fire and torture; came with death-dealing powder and ball, only in his methods of destruction superior to the Incas.

Where order had been, confusion reigned; where plenty had smiled, famine reared her ghastly head. Where justice had ruled, oppression and slavery bound men in chains. The superstition of idolatry gave way to the worse superstition of a perverted Christianity. The better idolatrous kingdom fell, and the so-called Christian kingdom followed; and of its civilization after four centuries, men are led to say, "South America oozes ignorance, superstition, and inefficiency in its masses."

Yet it would not be just to say that all Spaniards were like Francisco Pizarro, or his Dominican friar, Valverde, or the covetous, licentious lot that have followed them. There were priests of the Las Casas type, who longed to save men, and who wrote that strongest of indictments, in 1542, "Destruction of Indians." There were men like Mendoza, and Sarmiento, and Ondegardo, who were better than their creed, and who protested against the cruelty and wrong and injustice heaped upon those to whom everything belonged and who were robbed of everything, in the name of Christ. And there are noble men in South America who, protesting against the abuse of the Indian, continue to the present time, as Mr. Stahl discloses. We close this introduction in the words of a Spanish Roman Catholic who was with Pizarro. We copy from the *National Geographic Magazine* of May, 1916, page 521:

"True confession and protestation in the hour of death by one of the first Spaniards, conquerors of Peru, named Marcio Serra de Lejesama, with his will proved in the city of Cuzco on the fifteenth of November, 1589, before Geronimo Sanchez de Quesada, public notary.

"First, before beginning my will, I declare that I have desired much to give notice to his Catholic majesty King Philip, our lord, seeing how good a Catholic and Christian he is, and how zealous in the service of the Lord our

God, concerning that which I would relieve my mind of, by reason of having taken part in the discovery and conquest of these countries, which we took from the lords Yncas, and placed under the royal crown, a fact which is known to his Catholic majesty.

"The said Yncas governed in such a way that in all the land neither a thief, nor a vicious man, nor a bad, dishonest woman was known. The men all had honest and profitable employment. The woods, and mines, and all kinds of property were so divided that each man knew what belonged to him, and there were no lawsuits. The Yncas were feared, obeyed, and respected by their subjects, as a race very capable of governing; but we took away their land, and placed it under the crown of Spain, and made them subjects.

"Your majesty must understand that my reason for making this statement is to relieve my conscience, for we have destroyed this people by our bad examples. Crimes were once so little known among them that an Indian with one hundred thousand pieces of gold and silver in his house, left it open, only placing a little stick across the door, as the sign that the master was out, and nobody went in.

But when they saw that we placed locks and keys on our doors, they understood that it was from fear of thieves, and when they saw that we had thieves amongst us, they despised us. All this I tell your majesty, to discharge my conscience of a weight, that I may no longer be a party to these things. And I pray God to pardon me, for I am the last to die of all the discoverers and conquerors, as it is notorious that there are none left but me, in this land or out of it, and therefore I now do what I can to relieve my conscience."

The original Spanish is given in Prescott's "Peru," appendix 4, volume 2, page 335.

Evidently the horrible butcheries and treacheries did not weigh so heavily upon the conscience of the old soldier, as they were done in the name of Christ.

But light is breaking; and it is dawning not only in the minds of the Quichuas and the Aymaras, so long oppressed, but in the minds of the best men in Peru. The gospel of God does not compel, it persuades; it does not force compliance, it wins souls to life.

THE PUBLISHERS.

ANA and author FERNANDO STAHL

CHAPTER I

On the Roof of the World

"THE roughest port in all the world!" That is what one of the ship's officers said as we cast anchor at the port of Mollendo, Peru, after a voyage of twenty days from New York.

Just then appeared an interesting sight. Racing through the water were some thirty small boats, each containing two or three men, who were pulling wildly at their oars, trying to get to our ship first. Five or six boats reached the ship's ladder at the same time; but before they had touched the side of the vessel, the men were jumping upon the ladder, pushing and crowding one another as they bounded on board.

In another moment, there was an excited jabbering of Spanish at the passengers. The boatmen were all eager to help the passengers ashore, bag and baggage. We did not understand their speech, but were so fortunate as to have with us E. W. Thomann, who spoke the language, and who had made this trip before. He arranged with two of the men to take us ashore. They soon had our

(35)

Landing Place, Mollendo, "The Roughest Port in the World"

baggage in their boat; and after some little difficulty, we entered.

The waves were running high, and it seemed to me a miracle that we did not capsize. As we neared the landing, we saw some of the people hoisted onto the pier in a large chair hauled up by a hoisting engine. Our men, however, said they could land us without the aid of the engine; and after several desperate attempts, we finally managed to step upon the stair that extended into the water from the pier. We quickly passed through the customs, and boarding a train that was in waiting, were soon on our way to "the roof of the world."

Every foot of the way is upgrade; and the curves of the railroad are so sharp and numerous that some of the passengers became trainsick. For many hours, we traversed vast sandy wastes, passing great heaps of white sand, which we were told were the famous moving sand dunes of Peru. These sand dunes are crescent-shaped, over a hundred feet long, and from ten to twenty feet high; and one peculiar thing about them, owing to the prevailing winds, is that the crescent always lies in the same direction.

THE FAMOUS SAND DUNES BETWEEN MOLLENDO AND AREQUIPA, PERU

Just at dusk, our train pulled into Arequipa, a city of 40,000 inhabitants, situated about 7,000 feet above sea level. Here we were to stop overnight, as our train did not go on until the next morning. We secured lodgings near the station; and leaving my wife, daughter, and baby boy at the hotel, I went with Pastor Thomann to visit some of the people with whom he was acquainted. The narrow, winding streets contrasted strangely with the wide thoroughfares of the North American cities to which I had been accustomed.

After fifteen minutes' walk, we stopped at a low building, and rapped on the door. A stout, dark man appeared, who greeted us most profusely, throwing his arms about my friend first, then embracing me. I was rather embarrassed by this style of greeting, but it is quite usual in South America.

We were shown into the house, and while my fellow traveler and our host were carrying on a lively conversation in a tongue then unknown to me, I was looking about. On one side of the room in which we sat, was a bed occupied by some one who appeared to be very restless; and as soon as there was a lull in the conversation, I asked what ailed the person in the bed. The host answered, "Oh, that is one of my children, down sick with smallpox!" I was dumfounded. But I felt thankful that I had been vaccinated. I afterward learned that these people regard smallpox a great deal as some people in America

STREET MARKET, AREQUIPA, PERU, SHOWING THE FRUIT OF SOIL AND LOOM

regard measles. They say, "The sooner you have it, the better."

After a few moments, we bade our host good night, and made our way over the rough, dark road to the outskirts of the city, where the Harvard Observatory is located. An hour's hard walking through the darkness brought us to the place, and we spent a very pleasant two hours with Mr. Frank E. Hinckley, the superintendent of the institution. He proved to be a most affable man. He showed us about the observatory, explaining the workings of the huge telescopes; and we looked through some of them at the wonders of the heavens.

As we were making our way along the dark streets again to our lodgings, we heard the twanging of guitars at different places, as an accompaniment to what at that time I thought was the most horrible singing I had ever heard. The musicians were serenaders, who often spend most of the night in this way.

When we entered our hotel, there was an excited mob of people in the street; and we were told that during our absence, the hotel had caught fire. I found my family nearly exhausted from fatigue and the fire scare.

When the fire broke out, the people filled the place, all talking at once; and as the language was strange to my wife, she could not understand what was the matter, until she saw the smoke. Fortunately the blaze was put out, and very little damage was done.

STILL CLIMBING THE MOUNTAINS

The next morning at seven, amidst a great crowd of people, we boarded the train for Puno. We were surprised to find the train so crowded. About every place was taken, but finally we succeeded in getting seats. There was a tremendous amount of excited talking, which is a feature of Latin American life that always seems strange to us. As the bell sounded for the starting of the train, nearly every one on the train, to our great amazement, made a rush for the doors. It developed that there were very few passengers, but many friends to see off the few. As the train moved out, we adjusted our baggage, and found more comfortable seats.

Up to this time, we had not been conscious of any effects of the altitude; but after we reached an elevation of 12,000 feet, we began to feel uneasy. However, we blamed the cigarette smoke for this. Nearly every one smokes on the trains here. About three o'clock in the afternoon, when we had reached Crucero Alto, the highest point of the railway, 14,300 feet above sea level, we all began to have headaches, and some of the passengers were prostrated. The air became very cold, and we could breathe only with difficulty.

PUNO — DISCOURAGING OUTLOOK

Just at sundown, our train pulled into Puno, a town located on the shores of Lake Titicaca. We secured lodgings at the only hotel at that time in the little town, and were ready to retire, as we were suffering because of the altitude; but the proprietor insisted that we have some supper. He told us that we would feel a great deal better after eating. Accordingly, we were ushered into the dining room.

The first course served was some very hot soup — not so hot from the fire over which it had been cooked, as from the abundance of red pepper it contained. As the kitchen door leading to the dining room swung open, we beheld a sight that rather discouraged us from eating any more. The cook would throw the pans down on the floor when he had taken the food from them; and in a moment, they would be full of guinea pigs, which were eating the residue from the same pan in which our food had been cooked.

We were to stop at this place for two days to wait for a little steamer to take us across to the other side of the lake. The next morning, we took a stroll about the village; and never in our lives did we meet a more discouraging sight. The air was cold, the place looked very dreary, and the people seemed to be unsociable. My wife and daughter remarked, "Evidently we have come to the wrong place to do missionary work." Little did we think, at that time, that only a few years later, we should be privileged to open a mission for the Indians near this place. Early in the morning of the third day, we boarded the little steamer called "The Inca," which was to take us across the lake to Bolivia. The weather had changed, and never had we seen such bright sunshine. The air was so clear that one could easily see mountains over a hundred miles away.

Contrary to the usual idea, this region, although situated in the torrid zone, is always

MOUNT MISTI, A LIVE VOLCANO, AREQUIPA, PERU

too cool for comfort, because of the high altitude. The summers are wet and cold, and the winters dry and cold. The atmosphere is highly charged with electricity, which is very taxing on the nervous system; and the altitude requires one to have good heart and lungs. During the day, the thermometer indicates fifty degrees in the shade, while the sunshine is exceedingly warm. The nights, however, are bitterly cold, the mercury falling below the freezing point. These quick, severe changes are unhealthful, causing especially much catarrhal trouble.

The course of our tiny steamer followed the shore, giving us good opportunity to see the country. We were struck by its barrenness. There were no trees or vegetation anywhere in sight. We were right up in the heart of the great Indian country. Millions of Indians live on the table-land surrounding this lake. Thousands of little mud huts could be seen along the shore; and as we thought of the many thousands of these poor, neglected Indians, our hearts went out to them, and we prayed the prayer of Jabez — 1 Chronicles 4: 10 — that the Lord would enlarge our coasts, and enable us to do these people some good.

Lake Titicaca contains over four thousand square miles, being about the size of Lake Erie. It is the highest navigable lake in all the world, having an altitude of 12,490 feet

"La Balsa" (Straw Boat), Lake Titicaca

above sea level. The water of the lake is always icy cold. There are some fish in it about the size of perch, but they are not very numerous. Growing along the shore quite plentifully is a tall grass that the Indians call *tortori*. They feed this grass to their cattle, and also make very useful little boats from it, tying it in long bundles, then fastening these bundles together in such a way as to form a boat. The ropes with which the bundles are tied together are made from the tough mountain grass. The boats can be made very cheaply, and prove serviceable indeed to the Indians, as they are very buoyant. A sail also is made from the same material.

CHAPTER II

Inca Ruins and Traditions

THE history of these people is most interesting. Prescott's "History of Peru" deals quite fully with it. Tradition declares that the sun, taking pity upon the people in that highland region, sent his two children, Manco Capac and Mama Occlo, son and daughter, husband and wife, to found an empire for them. They took with them a golden wedge; and where this golden wedge would of itself sink into the ground and disappear from sight, they were to found the empire. As the two children were making their way through that mountain region, they tried the wedge at different places. Finally they arrived at Cuzco, and there the wedge sank from sight forever. Hence the Inca empire was founded at that place.

Manco Capac immediately set about instructing the men in the science of agriculture, while Mama Occlo took in hand the women, instructing them in the arts of spinning and weaving. Gaining the confidence of the people, they amalgamated the many different tribes into one great Inca empire.

(49)

AN ARCHWAY IN CUZCO
REPRESENTING THE MORE MODERN STYLE OF STONEWORK
The statue of a priest at the top indicates the domination of the Roman Catholic Church.

In the vicinity of Lake Titicaca, and in the highland region round about, are some extensive and remarkable ruins of temples, which are the remnant of the historic civilization that thrived in the time of the Incas. The stones used in the building of these temples are of enormous size, some of them weighing hundreds of tons each; and the marvel is, how the people were able to transport them from the distant quarries, up high mountain sides, down great cañons, and across rivers.

The walls of some of these Inca temples and fortresses are beautifully made. The stones exactly fit one another, no mortar or cement having been used to fasten them together. They are joined so nicely that one cannot insert the blade of a penknife between the edges of the stones, or even a needle at the corners of them. They are cut in many different shapes; and how the people could have hewed these massive stones with such exactness, supposedly having to move them about repeatedly to fit them together, is an unsolved mystery.

Here and there among these ruins are great carved idols, many of them of gigantic size, giving us an idea of what the religion of the

A WALL OF CORICANCHA, JOINTS IN MASONRY ALMOST INVISIBLE

people must have been. They worshiped the sun and the forces and objects of nature. Even to-day some of the Indians worship the sun, and many worship the earth.

These Indians live in small mud huts, about twelve feet long and ten feet wide, thatched with straw, without any windows, and with but a small opening for a door — so small that only with difficulty can one get through. They have earthen floors, and no furniture of any kind. Their clothes are hung on ropes and poles placed across the hut. On one side of the hut, the floor is elevated a little, and used for a bed.

The Indians spin and weave all their clothes. Those of a man usually consist of a shirt, a pair of trousers, which are slit up from the ankle to the knee in the back to facilitate his wading the numerous small mountain rivers, and a poncho, which is simply a large blanket, with a hole cut in the middle, through which he slips his head, the blanket falling over his shoulders. These ponchos generally are highly colored. To complete his costume, the Indian wears a small wool cap, with ear-laps that he pulls tightly over his head, and on top of this, a large, thick felt hat, which also the Indians themselves manufacture.

The clothes of the women consist of skirts made of wool, and a waist of the same material. On any special occasion, a woman puts on ten or twelve of these heavy skirts of different colors, one skirt being tied just a little higher than the preceding one, so as to show the color of the one beneath. The women wear hats that they themselves have devised. The framework is made of tough mountain grass, covered with navy blue cloth, and the rim is faced with red cloth. Underneath the hat is worn a light shawl of some colored material.

The diet of the Indians is rather monotonous. As no fruit grows in these high altitudes, the people live mostly on mutton, barley, potatoes, quinoa (a small grain of which they make porridge), and most important of all, *chuñas,* which are used extensively by all the Indians of the high plateaus. *Chuñas* are simply potatoes treated in a special way. After the harvest in the autumn, the potatoes are spread out on the plains, and left to freeze for about ten days. After that, they are thawed out, and then the Indian goes

INDIAN WOMAN WEAVING PONCHOS

out with his family, and they stamp upon the potatoes with their bare feet. When the water has all been thoroughly stamped out, they are removed to a dry place, and permitted to dry for about a week. After this process, the potatoes are called *chuñas*. About six bushels of potatoes make one bushel of *chuñas*. These are one of the staple articles of diet for the Indians, and are carried on long journeys, being of very light weight. They are also used in soups, and in every part of their diet, even flour being made of them. In so far as we have been able to find out, they are wholesome.

The majority of these Indians have little pieces of land they cultivate; and each family owns ten or fifteen sheep, which furnish them with meat to eat and wool for their clothing; and some of them own a cow or two. But the Indians that live in an altitude of over 13,000 feet do not cultivate their land, as nothing grows on these high ranges except a tough, yellow grass. These Indians have large herds of alpacas and llamas, from which they cut the wool, taking it to the lower altitudes to trade for foodstuffs.

Harvesting the Wool Crop from Alpacas

There are two tribes of these Indians, the Quichuas and the Aymaras. The Quichuas are far in the majority, there being fully six million of them in the three republics of Bolivia, Ecuador, and Peru. There are about five hundred thousand of the Aymaras in Peru and Bolivia. It is thought by some that the Aymaras are descendants of the Pre-Inca people, or as they are sometimes called, the Megalithic or "Big Stone" people, and the Quichuas, of the Incas.

These Indian languages are not easy to acquire. They are made up of many guttural sounds and clicks, and contain difficult combinations of consonants in the verbs. The words nearly all end in vowels, and nearly all are accented on the syllable next to the last. In its use of adjectives, and its facility for forming compound nouns, using the first noun adjectively, the language resembles English. Instead of prepositions, it has suffixes appended to the nouns and the pronouns, as in the old Anglo-Saxon words. The grammatical principles of the Aymara and the Quichua are practically the same, although the vocabularies differ greatly.

INCA RUINS AND TRADITIONS 59

A voyage of ten hours took us across the lake to the Bolivian side; and leaving our little steamer, we boarded a train that was in waiting to take us to La Paz, the largest city in the republic. After a few hours' ride over a great barren plain, our train stopped at "The Alto," and our locomotive was uncoupled for an electric motor, which was to take us down into La Paz. As we made the descent, a most wonderful view met our gaze. "A city in a kettle," La Paz is called. With its many colored roofs, situated at the head of a great cañon, bounded on three sides by majestic walls several thousand feet high, it makes a picturesque sight indeed.

Our electric train wound its way around and around down the mountain side, taking forty minutes to make the descent. At the station, we saw a unique and interesting spectacle,— the Spanish people, dressed in their somber black; the *cholos,* or mixed people, their women in very short dresses, with a great show of lace extending below, with their high-topped and high-heeled shoes, and their white Panama hats; and the hundreds of Indians, copper-colored, with black eyes and straight black hair, and wearing a profusion of colors. It has been truly said that no other city in all the world has such a show of colors as may be seen among the people of La Paz.

We engaged rooms, and took our baggage at once from the station. There were no drays nor express wagons. Everything had to be carried on the backs of the Indians, and really they are very efficient. An Indian will tie upon his back a large trunk weighing two hundred pounds, take a valise in each hand, and walk thus for miles.

As we were walking to our place of lodging, I found myself coming into collision with persons I met. It is the custom here, as in some European countries, to turn to the left on meeting a person, instead of to the right, as we do in the United States. It was a few days before I could accustom myself to this difference. Another peculiar usage here is that of waving the hand away from the body instead of toward it, in beckoning to a person. But we soon become accustomed to these changes.

Of the eighty thousand inhabitants of La Paz, sixty thousand are Indians, fifteen thousand are *cholos,* or the mixed class, and five

A Cholo Woman and Child

thousand are Spanish. The Spanish people make up the highest class, as doctors, lawyers, and officials, and are very well-to-do. The *cholos* are largely artisans, and could well be called the middle class; while the Indians are the laborers and the roustabouts,— the poorest class.

Neither the Spanish nor the *cholo* people are ever seen carrying any bundles, no matter how small. When they go out shopping, they have Indians following along behind them to carry whatever they may purchase. These Indians are the servants, and do all the cooking and the general housework.

Our greatest ambition now was to learn the language of the people. I was soon able to speak a few words in Spanish quite well — so well, in fact, that the people I addressed did not guess the limitations of my vocabulary, and sometimes proceeded to talk to me very sociably, though I had little idea of what they were saying. This made me feel uncomfortable, and I longed for the day when I could talk to the people and understand them.

It was decided that while Pastor Thomann was with me, we should go to Cochabamba, an interior city of Bolivia, to become acquainted with the conditions there. So after only a week's stay at La Paz, leaving my wife, daughter, and little son there, we started out to visit Cochabamba. We took a train to Oruro, a city located out on the barren plain of the mountains, without any protection whatsoever. Here we made arrangements for another two days' journey by coach to Cochabamba. Early the next morning, we started on our journey. The weather was bitterly cold, and the wind was blowing a gale. We had just seated ourselves in the large coach, when the driver, a half-breed, gave a savage yell, and the eight mules bounded off at a most furious rate, the driver whipping them unmercifully all the while. I could not endure seeing him whip the poor animals in this fashion, and leaned over the seat to ask him why he did so when they were going as fast as they possibly could. He made no answer. As we dashed over the plain, the driver still whipping the mules, I saw blood starting from their flanks. I shook him roughly, and told him he would have to stop beating those mules. He seemed very much surprised that any one should try to prevent him from pounding the mules; but as what I said was translated to him, he desisted somewhat.

After a few hours, we left the plain, and started down the mountain side, at times passing along a narrow ledge and curving around the mountain, all the while going as fast as the mules could gallop. Sometimes the heavy wheels of the coach would strike large stones in the road, that would send us bounding off our seat, our heads often striking on the ceiling of the coach. It was all new to me, and Pastor Thomann had many a good laugh at me as we went along. I queried whether the city we were going to had been named Cochabamba because of the banging of the coach on the way. Every two hours and a half, the mules were changed for fresh animals, and the driver would take a large glass of beer, and away we would go again at breakneck speed along the mountain side, or following the river bed.

The second evening, we pulled into Cochabamba. After securing lodging, we at once sought our beds, as we were very tired; but to my surprise, I passed a very restless night. Early in the morning, I found out why. I discovered that my hands and face were cov-

A Mountain Coach

ered with great welts, and I asked the Indian servant what was the cause of these. He beckoned me to the wall on one side of the room, and pointed into the large crevices, making me understand that the red bugs I saw there were what had been disturbing my sleep, and were the cause of these welts on my hands and face. They were horrible looking objects, some of them as large as my thumb, a sword-like beak over a quarter of an inch long protruding from their heads, and their great red bodies swollen with the blood they had taken from me. The Indian called them *pinchugas*. He said that their bite was poisonous, and that I should use some medicine to wash with. This I did, and felt somewhat relieved. We stayed long enough for me to become acquainted with the people at Cochabamba with whom my predecessor had worked in evangelistic lines.

The thing that impressed me most in this place was the many hundreds of priests walking up and down the streets, and the homage the people offered them, many kneeling before them and kissing their hands as they went along the streets. There are thousands of Quichua Indians in this province; and on market days, Thursdays and Sundays, many come into the city to sell their wares. I would have liked to stay longer at this place, to study the people, but could not do so on this occasion. After a few days, we tried to get seats in the coach to return to Oruro; but this was impossible, all the seats having been engaged for weeks ahead. The best we could do was to ride on top of the baggage wagon, among boxes and bundles; but as the mules galloped along the uneven road, we had all we could do to keep from being jolted off. We were completely covered with dust and dirt, and I was sincerely glad when we could bid good-by to that conveyance.

At Oruro, Pastor Thomann left me to continue my journey alone to La Paz, and he went to his own field of labor in Chile. I felt very lonely when we separated, as he had been a good companion, and was also a great help to me because of his knowledge of Spanish.

On returning to La Paz, I found that both my wife and my daughter had suffered a very severe illness, having had mountain fever. It was some time before my wife became accustomed to the high altitude and the rigorous mountain climate.

CHAPTER III

A Primitive People

WHILE studying the language, we visited among the people, and sold Bibles and other religious books, by this latter means meeting many of the expenses of our missionary work.

We were mostly interested in the Indians, and after a few months, moved into a great Indian neighborhood called Challyapampa, in the suburbs of La Paz. We opened a free dispensary there, and tried to help the Indians in every way, but we found them very conservative. Spanish women used to stand at our gate, and forbid the Indians to come to us. They called us offensive names, and told the Indians that we were very bad people. We could not defend ourselves very well, because we could not speak the language.

I determined that while I was studying the language, I would visit the Indians in the great tropical region of Bolivia. So I bought a saddle horse and two pack mules, and made four strong boxes, which I filled with Bibles, other books, and magazines; and one morn-

INDIANS OF SOUTH AMERICA

ing at two o'clock, I started out to visit this great forest region of Bolivia. My first day's journey took me over the high, barren mountains; and that evening, I reached Pongo, some thirty-five miles distant from La Paz. I was very tired, not being accustomed to horseback riding.

Pongo is an Indian name which means *door*. At this place, there was a *tambo,* or hotel, where travelers could stay for the night. It consisted of several low structures built of mud and thatched with straw, and divided into four rooms about ten by ten feet in size. In each room was a wooden bench, which the proprietor called a bed, but no bedding whatever. The earthen floor was bare, and there were no windows, and there was only a small opening for a door. There were several large yards, or corrals, about thirty by forty feet in size, with high walls around them, in which horses and mules were kept.

The meals consisted of about three courses, each successive one being more peppery than the preceding, and necessitating large draughts of water to put out the fire the food seemed to kindle in the stomach.

All together, the hotels in these countries are very uninviting. I came to prefer sleeping out on the open plain, bringing my own food with me, if possible, and thus avoiding these dreary places.

The next day, I got another early start. In a short time, the road descended so rapidly that my horse was compelled to slide two and three feet at a time. The way now led through a heavy forest, and the Indians I met stopped and eyed me as far as they could see me, evidently surprised at my being alone. People said it was dangerous for me to make the trip thus; but I had no one to go with me. My Spanish teacher had prevailed upon me to take his rifle, telling me that the mere fact of my having it in sight would afford more safety, as there were robbers in those regions.

Toward evening, the air became a great deal warmer, as I reached a much lower altitude. I began looking for a place where I could stop for the night, hoping to be able to retire early, as I was very tired from riding and walking alternately over the rough roads.

About five-thirty in the afternoon, I came to a large house, where I asked, in my broken Spanish, if I could stay overnight. The man with whom I spoke said he had no place for me, but that I would find one a little farther along the road. I kept on for several hours, but found no place to stay, and it became very difficult to keep the way in the darkness. I had just about made up my mind to stop on the road for the night, when I heard some one coming toward me, and called out to inquire if he knew where I could get feed for my animals and a place to sleep. An Indian answered in his own language. I did not understand what he said, but I quickly followed him. He led the way into an opening through the forest, off the road; and in a few moments, we came to a fire around which some Indians were sitting. I made them understand that I wanted feed for my horse and mules, and they gave me some. Then I asked for food for myself, and offered money in payment for it; but they refused the money, telling me they hardly had food for themselves.

I seated myself near them, and taking up a little Indian child about two years old, started to pet it and talk to it, and gave it a few trinkets that I had. This seemed to please the Indians immensely, and one of them immediately arose and brought me some food. After-

AN ORDINARY PERUVIAN ROAD

ward I gave them several pamphlets with pictures on the covers, and they appeared to be very much interested in these pictures. Soon I was rolled up in my blanket, fast asleep.

The next morning, I awoke early. The Indians helped me to put my boxes on the mules again, and I continued on my way. The road was rougher than ever. About noon, I came to a place unusually narrow and steep, leading along the face of a great cliff. There was a precipice hundreds of feet deep on one side, and a wall of solid rock on the other.

As I was going up this steep trail, I noticed that on ahead, a great stone had been washed out, leaving a perpendicular rise of about three feet in the narrow trail. For a moment, I was dismayed, and wanted to turn back. But I could not do so, because of the narrowness of the way; so I had to go on. I called loudly to the leading mule, and he jumped up the ascent, as also did my saddle horse; but the last animal, which was loaded heavily with books, did not succeed, and started to fall over backward. I gave a desperate pull at the rope on the side of his head;

and he seemed to receive a push from unseen hands, for he recovered his balance, and cleared the awful place.

When I told some of the people in the next town, about that experience, they said: "We know the place. The hand of Providence was surely with you." And I know it was.

About three o'clock that afternoon, I came to a small house by the roadside; and I asked an Indian who was standing near, if he would sell me some oranges. I gave him five cents, and he immediately left me. He was gone fully half an hour, and I almost gave up his returning; but just as I was about to start on my way again, I saw him coming, struggling along under a great gunny sack filled with oranges. He had brought me fully a hundred and fifty pounds of oranges for the five cents. I was amazed. I took all that I could carry in my saddlebags and pockets, and told him to keep the rest. I did not understand his generosity, until I had gone about a half mile farther down the road. There the branches of the orange trees hung above my head, laden with fruit, which I could have picked easily while going along on horseback.

I reached the town of Corroico in the evening, and I determined to stay in this place for a few days. I put my horse and mules into a pasture for a rest, and started out the next day to sell Bibles and magazines. The first man I met was the priest of the town; and when I showed him our books and magazines, he asked what denomination I represented. I answered, "The Seventh-day Adventist."

"Seventh-day Adventist!" he said. "What does that mean?"

I told him "Seventh-day" means that we keep the seventh day, the Bible Sabbath, which has existed from the time when the Lord created the earth; and that as Adventists, we believe in the second coming of Christ.

"Oh," he said, "that's it, huh? Well, that isn't so very much different from what we believe. Although we do not keep the seventh day, we believe in it just the same." He put his name down on my list. I then started out to visit the other people of this village. As I showed them our papers and books, they would shake their heads, and say they did not want them. Then I would show them the signature of the priest, and tell them how he

INDIAN OF THE TROPICS OF THE YUNGAS OF BOLIVIA

had recommended the publications, and almost every one would buy. I sold, in a few hours, over fifty magazines, and a number of Bibles and other books.

After a few days, I continued my journey into the interior of the great Yungas region. My next stop would be Coripata, the village farthest in the interior. The Indians of this section all wear their hair in one long braid hanging down the back. They are of slenderer build than the Indians of the high plateaus, and have slanting eyes, thin faces, and high cheek bones. They wear short knee breeches, and very small hats. They seem to be very ignorant, none of them speaking Spanish, and most of them being addicted to the use of alcoholic drinks. I found that they were employed for the most part upon the large plantations of the Spaniards, working three days each week for the *patron,* as they call the landlord, for the privilege of living upon a small plot of ground, which they can work for themselves the remaining part of the week.

After having gone about fifteen miles, I met a very rough-looking man mounted on a mule. As he passed me, he said, in Spanish,

"*Guarde de los fangos.*" I did not know the meaning of the word *fangos;* but because of the man's serious tone, I expected to encounter nothing less than a tiger or a boa constrictor. I thanked him, unslung the rifle my Spanish teacher had lent me, saw that it was in good working order, and made my way forward. I had gone about a quarter of a mile when I came upon — not a tiger nor a boa constrictor, but a place where a landslide had occurred, obliterating a section of the road for almost its entire width. The narrow path that remained was very steep, and the soft mud added to the danger of slipping down the mountain side. I knew now what *fango* was, and I have never forgotten it — *mud!*

I dismounted and waded carefully across the dangerous place, about thirty feet wide. I then got a mule across. He stumbled through all right. Next came my saddle horse and the other mule. In a few minutes, we were all safely across. After I had scraped most of the mud off, I continued my journey, reaching Coripata that evening just before dusk, without any further mishaps. I asked several persons if there was a place for travelers to stay overnight; but they answered very surlily, "No." I tried to get food for my beasts, but did not succeed, so went to the main plaza, and prepared to spend the night there.

Just then an Indian came running to me with a letter, which I found to be an invitation to spend the night at the home of the man who wrote it. I immediately followed the Indian, and he led me to a beautiful place near the village. The family were very friendly; and the man proved to be a senator from La Paz, who was spending a few months here at his summer home. He appeared to be much interested as I explained to him our mission to that country, and what we were endeavoring to do for the people, especially the Indians.

In the morning, my host offered me a guide as far as the river. I was afterward glad I accepted, because we had not gone far when the trail became very uncertain, and it grew more and more indistinct as we proceeded. After a few hours, we came to a large river. My guide pointed out the place to land on the other side, and left me. It was with difficulty that I was able to ford this river, as the cur-

A Natural Cut

rent was strong, and the water was deep in places. I crossed safely, however, but found that the trail was hardly visible on the other side, because of the thick underbrush. I was afraid of losing my way altogether; and to be lost in these thick forests would be a dangerous situation. I prayed that God would keep me on the right way, then I let one of my mules go ahead. Many a time that day, this leading mule would take a course that I felt sure was wrong. I would try to stop him to turn him back, but could not catch up with him, so had to follow on after him. At times, deer would spring into view. It was an altogether wild country.

Late that afternoon, to my delight, I came to an open place where there was a village. I made arrangements to stay with the man who kept the general merchandise store of the place. His son could speak English, having been in the United States for five years. They were very amiable.

The next day, I started out to sell books and magazines, and was so successful that I sold nearly all I had brought with me. That evening, however, people began to come to me and demand the return of their money, saying that the priest had told them the books were very bad. I asked what there was that was bad in the books, and I refused to return the money, telling the people they would be very glad afterward to have those books. While some left, others came, and soon groups were standing out in the street threatening me. I concluded that the best thing for me to do was to leave that place as soon as possible. I settled with my host before retiring, and told him I was going to leave very early the next morning.

I was up at two o'clock, and started off before three; but early as it was, people had already gathered on the plaza, and were talking excitedly. I paid no attention to them, however, but kept on my way. As I reached the outskirts of the town, I heard a loud calling. I felt sure that the people were coming out after me, so I did not turn around, but continued on at an even pace. The calling became louder and louder, and finally I turned about. Then a man dashed up and told me that I was taking the wrong road to La Paz. I felt relieved, and thanked the man most heartily, and turned and went the road he directed me to take, which proved to be the right one.

That night, I stopped at a place called Yauacacha, one of the most beautiful places I saw in the whole Yungas region, or during the entire trip. I was much impressed with the great possibilities for the Indians here, who seemed to be more intelligent than those I had seen elsewhere; and I felt that for us to open an industrial Indian school at this place, if we could, would be a wise move. I sold all the papers and books I had; and the following day, I continued my way back to the city of La Paz, which I reached in a few days.

I had improved considerably in my knowledge of the Spanish language, and had more courage to work in behalf of the people. I could even speak a few words of the Indian language, and immediately I renewed my efforts for the Indians that lived about us. We visited from house to house, offering help where there was sickness.

Connected with our cottage, we had about an acre of ground, which we had planted to barley for use as horse feed. It sprouted nicely, but we found difficulty in getting water to irrigate it; for as soon as we would turn the water on, the Indians would turn it from its course again. We finally gave up the attempt.

About this time, a chief living in the neighborhood sent for us to treat him, as he was very ill of fever. I nursed him day after day for several weeks, and had the satisfaction of seeing him get well. One day, soon after his recovery, I saw water coming down toward us; and thereafter it continued to come until we were almost flooded, and I had to beg the Indians to shut it off.

Mrs. Stahl devoted a great deal of her time to the Indian women and children, also nursing in the homes of the best people of Bolivia and Peru. She went from the hovels of the Indians to the palaces of the rich, thus gaining for us many powerful friends among people of influence, who afterward favored us in our work for the Indians.

Our daughter, Frenita, who was sixteen years old at this time, and of a very cheery disposition, did much to break down the prejudice of the Indians. She visited their homes, and took a special interest in their little children, often bringing them home with her, and giving them dainties, thus winning their friendship and good will. Many a time she would say to her mother, "Wouldn't it be a pretty child if it were clean?" Then she would proceed to clean it up, and prove her opinion to be true. She was a curiosity to the Indians, with her blond hair and blue eyes. Even our little boy, Wallace, found a place in the work. He quickly learned the Indian language, and acted as interpreter for us.

A Child of Peru

CHAPTER IV

Missionary Mining

AFTER we had been in Bolivia for a year, a prominent American called upon me, and asked if I would go upon a mining expedition for him into the interior of Bolivia. I told him that I did not understand anything about mines, and that I was a missionary.

"Well," he said, "that is just the reason why I want you to go, as I feel confident you will bring back the right samples and a true report." I asked him if I could do missionary work for the people on the way. He assured me that I could do as I might choose. I then consented to go, and he immediately placed in my hands several hundred dollars to fit out the expedition. He told me to put in a good supply of food, as the way was long, and to make myself as comfortable as I could during the journey. I obeyed him implicitly in this, and bought a liberal supply of canned goods; so we ate New York food in the jungles of Bolivia on this journey. The owner of the mine which my friend expected to purchase accompanied me.

At every stop, I was able to help some sick person. At noon of the first Friday, I began to look for a place to spend the Sabbath. We went mile after mile without finding such a place. Nothing but the great mountain wilds greeted the eye.

About four-thirty that afternoon, we passed an Indian hut in the woods, by the side of a river. I wanted to stop, but was strongly advised by the owner of the mine not to do so. He said that these Indians were very savage, and that we were in danger of being killed. He said also that there was no food for us or the beasts at this place. So we went on.

We had not gone far when we met some traders coming toward us. Of these we inquired if there was a place where we could stop farther down. They answered: "No; the Indians are very savage, and will not even give you feed for your beasts, and will not permit you to stop with them. You will have to keep on going for another twelve hours."

The mine owner said, "I told you so."

"Well," I replied, "I am going back to that Indian hut we passed."

"It's no use," he protested.

But I insisted, so we returned. On arriving, I asked an Indian woman at the door if we might stop at their place, and if they would sell us feed for our mules.

"You may stop," she said, "and we can provide for your mules."

While we were unloading our goods, the woman prepared food for us, and tried in every way to make us comfortable. The mine owner was very much surprised. He said he had always understood that the Indians on this part of the road were savage.

"The Lord has provided a place for us," I told him.

Sabbath morning, the mine owner said, "Come, let us be going."

"My friend," I replied, "you forget what I told you yesterday,— that we would rest over Sabbath."

"Well, then," he said, "I will go on alone."

"Very well," I answered; "but I advise you to stay with me and enjoy a Sabbath blessing."

"All right! I will," he replied.

I then told the woman of the house about the Sabbath, and asked if we might stay until Sunday morning.

"Indeed you may," she said.

About ten that morning, the husband of the woman returned, and he as well as his wife tried to make us feel at home. In a few hours, other Indians had gathered. I talked to them of God, what He requires of us, and of the soon coming of our Lord Jesus; and I found willing listeners among them. At times, tears forced a way down their weather-beaten cheeks. Just as the sun began to go down behind the mountains, we had a most precious meeting, and the Indians felt free to ask questions. Even the mine owner was deeply affected, and would exclaim every once in a while: "What Indians! I never would have believed it of them."

Very early Sunday morning we continued on our journey. The Indians made us accept some fruit; and as we were about to start, the one with whom we had stayed, with his wife and son, came to me, and said: "Brother, our ears have heard a sweet message. Our hearts are full. We are glad to hear that Jesus is coming soon; and from this time, we are going to keep the commandments of God and the Sabbath." They begged me most pathetically to visit them again soon, and teach them

ALTAR ON THE SUMMIT OF ONE OF THE HIGHEST MOUNTAINS

the Bible. We then parted. These people had accepted God's message with joy and without hesitation.

A few days afterward, we reached the village of Suri, where the mine was located, five days from La Paz. Suri is a little village, situated on the top of high mountains at the head of a fertile valley, in a thickly inhabited region. The people soon learned that I had a knowledge of the care of the sick, and they began to bring their sick to me. One woman brought a baby from a distance of twenty miles. I was very busy day after day, treating these poor heathen people. I made it a point to pray with them all, and while treating the sick, would explain to them the lovingkindness of God and the Lord Jesus Christ.

I was so busy that I almost forgot to get the samples I had come for. I stayed there five days, and the last day was the busiest of all. By that time, the people who had been treated the first few days were well on the road to recovery. I then visited the mine, securing samples of ore at different places, making drawings of the locations, taking photographs of the region, and locating them on the map that I had made. After a few more days, I was ready to return to La Paz.

The morning I was to leave, as I was getting ready to mount my mule, I found that the whole village had turned out to say "Good-by." One of the leading men said: "We have enjoyed your visit. You have done us good. You are different from the mining men we have met in the past. If you come here with your family, we will build you a house. We want to accept your religion. It is much better than what we have had. We want to keep the Sabbath. We have kept no day in the past." One old man told me he would give me a gold mine if I would return.

It seems that the Lord prepares the people for His message; for when we tell them of the soon coming of the Saviour, and of the importance of being ready, we seldom find any who do not feel that it is the truth, and want to make preparation to meet Him by putting the evil out of their lives.

Every one of the people had brought fruit, and asked me to take it along with me; but this was impossible. I picked out a little of the choicest, and thanked the people very much for their kindness, and told them that

I hoped to be back some day and teach them more.

We returned to La Paz by a different route from that by which we came; but in a few days, I was sorry that we did, for this road led us through a very rough part of the country. In many places, it was steep and dangerous. We had to ford boiling mountain torrents, and with difficulty could we keep our mules from being washed down the stream.

The second day of the return journey, we came to a place where the road seemed to end. We looked about for the road on which to continue, but found none. There were precipices all around us. Only one place seemed to be passable, and that led into a roaring torrent that ran between two huge cliffs. We could not see what was beyond; but as again and again we searched for a place to get out, and could find none, we decided to plunge into this wild torrent, with the hope of coming out on the other side all right. So we waded in. The terrific current instantly whirled our mules off their feet, and we were washed in between the cliffs. After a few moments, which seemed hours to me, we came to an

MISSIONARIES GREETED WITH FLAGS BY THE QUENUANI SCHOOL

(95)

opening on the other side of the gorge. There was a sharp turn in the river bed, and we were thrown violently out upon the shore.

We continued as fast as possible in the direction of La Paz. Early and late we were on the road. Our route now lay for the most part up steep mountain sides. About three o'clock one morning, while it was still dark, we were picking our way up the mountain, when I noticed that my mule had left the narrow, zigzag trail. At a point where he should have turned, he had kept right on, going out on the side of the cliff; and when I discovered that we were off the trail, we had already reached a place so steep that I was afraid to attempt to turn the mule around. I carefully stopped him and dismounted. It was with difficulty that I could keep my balance, and I gave up all hopes of saving the animal; but as I was wondering whether possibly I could get the saddle and bridle off and save them, suddenly the mule turned around and quietly and meekly made his way back to the road. I quickly followed him, very thankful for our marvelous escape, and we continued our journey.

When we were one day's ride from the city of La Paz, I became very ill. That night, when we stopped at a house, I was hardly able to dismount. I had violent chills and fever all night. Early the following morning, I got up with difficulty, mounted my mule, and continued my journey as rapidly as possible.

On arriving at La Paz, I turned over my samples and maps to the man who had sent me to investigate the mine. I lay in bed for three weeks after that, with malaria.

CHAPTER V

Exigencies of Missionary Pioneering

THE calls made upon us by the people were now almost more than we could meet; so we were made glad when we received notice that Brother Ignacio Kalbermatten and his wife were coming from Argentine to help us. As soon as they arrived, we began to hold meetings for the Indians, in the streets of La Paz, speaking through an interpreter. One result of these meetings was that a Spanish woman of a well-to-do La Paz family, who understood the Indian language, accepted the gospel message.

A few months after the arrival of these first coworkers, Brother Otto Schultz came to relieve us of the book work. We were very thankful for this additional help, as our work had become very heavy. We still continued our dispensary work for the Indians, Mrs. Stahl having charge of this department.

As we were working in this way, Mrs. Stahl became suddenly ill of typhus fever, which proved to be very serious indeed. For weeks

STREET SCENE IN LA PAZ

she was in delirium. Two physicians, friends of mine, who called every day, told me plainly that she was beyond all human help. But our trust was in Him who knows no defeat; and eventually, to the wonder of our friends, she began to improve.

As it is very difficult to recover one's strength in these high altitudes after a severe illness, I decided to take Mrs. Stahl down to the *Yungas* regions, in order that she could recuperate. Accordingly, as soon as she was able to ride a horse, I fitted out the expedition, and with our son, we started. But we had overcalculated Mrs. Stahl's strength; and on the second day, I was compelled to lift her off her horse many times, in order that she might rest. To make matters worse, a heavy rain came on, and continued nearly all that day. We were not prepared for this rain, and consequently our clothing was wet through in a short time. Still we kept on, hoping to make our destination soon. By this time, Mrs. Stahl was suffering so much pain and fatigue that she could not refrain from weeping. That afternoon, we reached the *finca,* or farm, where we were to stay a few weeks. After the first week, Mrs. Stahl was able to take little walks out among the orange trees.

The afternoon of the fourth day, I received a telegram from La Paz, urgently requesting my return, because of the sickness of Brother Schultz. He had been taken down with typhoid fever, and was having hemorrhages. It was decided that I should leave at once for La Paz, to care for him.

The next morning, I started out early, leaving my wife, our little son, and our Indian boy at the *finca*. I traveled all that day, urging my mule forward as rapidly as possible, and nearly all of the following night, and reached La Paz early in the morning. I found Brother Schultz very ill. He was having convulsions, and needed the most careful attention; but after the third week of his sickness, we had the satisfaction of seeing him recover. Then I started out to meet my wife, who was coming in from the *Yungas* region.

About this time, I received a letter from Elder A. N. Allen, of Lima, Peru, asking me to meet him on the other side of Lake Titicaca and visit the Indians with him. I sent back word that I would meet him on the date designated. When I reached Puno, Peru, where we were to meet, I found that he had already gone into the interior. He had left word, however, where I was to meet him. I secured a horse, and early that morning started to the place. After going about fifteen miles, I saw Indians coming toward me on horseback. They approached rather shyly, and asked if I was the missionary that was coming to visit them. When told that I was, they said they had come to meet me, and would accompany me to their place. When I reached Plateria, I found Brother Allen there, also a great concourse of Indians.

The chief of these Indians, whose name was Camacho, had been there for the past three or four months, trying to interest his people in the better things of life. He was a very intelligent man, and was one of the few Indians who could read. He had come into possession of some of our Spanish publications that had been distributed through that region by Pastor Thomann; and through them he had become interested in the gospel.

As soon as he had read this literature, he began to teach his people what he had learned from it. In this way, he created an active interest among the Indians in the immediate

A PERUVIAN MOUNTAINEER

neighborhood. After a few months, as this interest grew, he wrote to our mission office at Lima, requesting that a teacher be sent to them. This led to Pastor Allen's visit, and his invitation to me to join him there.

I had long been especially interested in the Indians, and now I felt that the time had come when I should give my full time to them. I asked our South American Union Conference to release me from my Bolivian work, that I might come and live among the Indians on this side of the lake. Consent was given after a while, and my family and I have ever since devoted ourselves wholly to the Indians.

CHAPTER VI

An Oppressed Race

WE found the Indians in a truly deplorable condition, living in the most abject squalor and ignorance, knowing nothing whatever of the simplest laws of hygiene, and addicted to the most horrible drunkenness, and to the cocaine habit.

Their little mud huts were filthy in the extreme, and full of vermin. On one side of the room usually was a small stove made of stones; and when the Indians cooked their meals upon these stones, the little room would be filled with smoke, which caused much disease of the eyes. They did not know the use of knives, forks, or spoons, but ate their food with their unwashed fingers.

They never bathed nor changed their clothes. We saw children there that had their clothes sewed upon them, it never being intended that the garments should be removed till they actually fell off because of decay due to the filth.

The Indians were beaten and deceived on every hand by the white people. They were considered as of less value than beasts. The

Indian Woman Grinding Barley

(106)

first to mistreat them were the great landowners, who for many years had systematically robbed them of their lands. These lands were originally taken by the Spanish *conquistadores,* who in turn contracted with many of the Indians to work in the mines, paying them in land. At that time, the land was regarded as of little worth; but it has proved to be valuable, being excellent grazing land for the alpaca, the llama, and the vicuña, whose natural habitat is on these high plateaus.

Any Indian who was strong and fortunate enough to endure the hard work of the mines for two or three years received a title to a large tract of land. These papers either have been lost, or have become unreadable because of great age; therefore in the suits with the powerful landowners, the Indians cannot prove their ownership by written titles, and most of the best lands have been taken from them.

The system of the usurpers was as effective as it was simple. Usually they forcibly removed the boundaries of the Indians' land, and at the same time laid claim to it. If an Indian remonstrated with a landowner, he was beaten by the landowner's servants. Finally the Indian in desperation would go to one of the larger villages and secure a lawyer to take his case in hand. This would necessitate a suit against the wealthy landowner. The lawyer would take the case, promising faithfully to present the necessary papers before the court, and get the return of the land. Many papers would be prepared, for each of which a charge of from one to four dollars would be made; and the Indian, in order to get money to pay for them and carry on the suit, would be obliged to sell his cattle.

For months, the Indian would go back and forth from his little hut to the distant village, inquiring of the lawyer how his case was proceeding. Usually the lawyer would encourage him, telling him that he had not lost the case, although he had not won it yet. At last, the lawyer would say that the Indian had won the case, that the land was his, and then would demand four or five dollars for making out the final papers. The Indian would return to his home, happy that he had won back his land, only to find, a few days later, that another suit had been instituted against him. He would go again to the lawyer, who would tell him: "Yes, such and such a man has now begun suit against you, and laid claim to your land, and we shall have to make out some papers and fight this man. We shall win, however."

Though the Indians have won the suits against the landowners again and again, still other suits have been brought against them immediately. In this way, an Indian would keep on until he had spent all his money, selling his cattle and everything he owned to defend himself, and after all lose his homestead. When an Indian was worn out and discouraged, the landowner would tell him that he might keep his place if he would take care of a few cattle for the landowner. The Indian, having no way to turn, would consent to this, and would take care of the cattle, his wife and children also working certain days for the landowner, helping in the planting and harvesting of the crops. After a year or so, the landowner would move the Indian and his family to a distant part of his large farm; and from that time, they would be literally absorbed by the landowner, who would see to it that the Indian was always in debt to him, and therefore never able to leave the farm. The Indians, not knowing how to keep accounts, could never clear themselves of debt, and were thus kept virtually in slavery. There were hundreds of Indians in this condition.

In *El Comercio,* a newspaper published in Lima, Peru, the following editorial on this subject appeared November 27, 1913:

"OUTRAGES SUFFERED BY NATIVE INDIANS

"Yesterday afternoon twenty-two natives from the provinces of Lampa and Azángaro came to this printing office, introduced by Sergeant Major Teodomiro Gutiérrez. These natives came to present a complaint; and with most somber colors, and phrases filled with emotion, they painted a distressing picture of the innumerable taunts, tortures, and robberies from which they are suffering.

"Far from bringing a vague charge, which would make their protest also vague, they bring, engraved in their memories, the names, dates, and places where these abuses have been perpetrated against them.

"The first to speak was a strapping youth, Avelino Zumi, of Lampa. He relates a tale of horror and spoliation. From him, as from nearly all his companions, have been taken

A "Finca" (Farm) in the Cuzco Valley

lands, small, to be sure, but upon which are founded all their hopes of a livelihood. The vicious system of feigned sales is employed; and these natives, being poor and despised and ignorant, cannot protest, within the boundaries of their own provinces, and get justice against such outrages. So they have to make immense sacrifices, and take long, hard journeys to Lima, such as this made by the twenty-two natives who are in this company, to find others who will hear their complaints and so remedy the evil which, in those sections distant from the capital, has grown to be a constant and odious system of oppression.

"Such complaints, it is true, have no new sound. It is a deep, uniform voice, which comes from many thousands of unfortunates deprived of their rights, and forced into all forms of slavery — a voice which is raised and which wishes to be heard on the road of rectitude, that reason may speak to conscience, rather than have to resort to insurrection, and stain with blood the fields which they inherited, and which are being taken from them to their deepest grief, the infamy being disguised under a maze of legal papers whose meaning they are not able to understand.

"Before such a tale of extortions, the question naturally arises, Why do they not make reclamation?

"But the fact is, there is no one to whom they can appeal; and we repeat it, they are compelled to come to Lima, and go directly and personally to the president of the republic, as these are now doing and others have done, to secure relief from the evils that afflict them.

"The preponderant power which the landlords have in each province, and their natural defenses when threatened, all the patronage whereby they farm out every small interest in the villages, itself as cruel as it is absurd, has generally succeeded in supplying the guaranties necessary to the enjoyment of the impunity which they demand.

"Avelino Zumi tells us: 'We have no one before whom we may make complaint; judges, subprefects, all are in with the landlords. Every protest, then, falls to the ground before the inactivity of the authorities, before the inertia of the judges; and when the cry becomes louder than usual, then comes the scorn of repression, penalties, ill treatment, the iron bar of the prison, and new abuses to terrorize the humble spirit of the natives.'

"Zumi continues telling us that no authority of the province of Lampa, nor any of the province of Azángaro, nor the department officers of Puno, have been able to put a stop to the excesses.

"Then he goes on telling us of another outrage: In the fore part of last May, several groups of natives went to the prefect of Puno, and this authority sent them to the subprefect of Lampa; but on reaching this place, though defenseless, they were attacked by the landlords and their followers with rifles and revolvers, and in that brutal attack, with all its odious characteristics of perfidy and savagery, five natives were killed and as many more wounded. But this was not enough. One of the wounded was taken by the assailants and carried away to the town of Taraco, province of Huancané, and there slain. It has not been possible even yet to determine the place where the body was buried.

"In another place, and always protected by that same impunity of which we have already spoken, the landlords not long ago declared the Indians had started an insurrection, though it did not exist save in the minds of those who concocted the malicious accusation. Then the authorities were stirred up, and forty-seven natives were thrown into prison in Samán, and ninety-seven in the remaining districts.

"Nor is that all. These prisoners are treated with a rigor beyond explanation; they are not permitted to receive even the food brought them by their fellow villagers. Many have died, others are sick, and of course they are not cared for.

"There is yet another cruel story: Last October, in the town of Achalla, Azángaro, the house of the native Andrés Apaza was attacked; he was wounded, and one of his young daughters, twelve years old, was first assaulted and then handcuffed. As the assailants fled, they set fire to the house, and the youngest daughter, Inocencia Apaza, was made fuel for the flames.

"To continue the narrative is but to relate more horrors. Greater inhumanity, or greater crime, is not conceivable, nor a greater abandonment. The natives of those lands, as it is, live at the mercy of the voracity of those men who brutally take possession of their property by violence, and of their lives by terror.

"The twenty-two natives who came yesterday, of whom we are speaking, make charges of the abuses related, and of others, against the following persons: Mariano Zuñiga Béjar, Ildefonso Gonzáles, Eloy Gonzáles, Telésforo Gonzáles, Luis Gonzáles, of Lampa; Francisco Ayamamana, steward of the Gonzáles family, from the same province; Manuel María Pérez, also of this province; Justo Romero, of Calavilla; Fabio Romero, from the same place; Mario Pérez, of Puyuse; Juan Yambe, from Samán; Juan Dereda, of Caminaca; Mariano Abarca Dueñas, from Samán; Miguel Salinas and Isidora Portugal, of Chupas, and from this place also, Francisco Paredes; Asunción, widow of Valcárcel and Manuel María Pérez, of Caracoto; and the priest Diego Castillo, of the same place.

"For his part, Sergeant Major Teodomiro Gutiérrez, who has just completed a commission of investigation in the southern departments concerning these same outrages from which the natives have suffered, for which commission he was appointed by the government, assures us of the truthfulness of the acts which these natives have come to us to denounce, and he declares that greater crimes are being committed by the landlords and by the authorities themselves.

"Surely the government, before whom these natives from Azángaro and Lampa will go to present themselves to-day or to-morrow, will apply an urgent remedy to so painful a situation, granting to the claimants the guaranties they ask, and, at the same time, ordering the restitution of the lands and other property which have been torn from them, and the punishment of the guilty."

As these Indians go through the villages on their way to the market to sell their little produce, the people of the village beat them and abuse them in many ways. If one of the villagers happens to want a messenger to go to some distant place, or has work to be done, the Indian is stopped in the street, and his goods are taken from him, and retained until he has delivered the message or done the work desired.

At other times, if a villager or a landowner wants to take his produce to some city to sell, and does not have enough burros and llamas for the purpose, he sends out his servants among the Indians, and forcibly borrows llamas and burros. After using these animals, sometimes for a week or two, he returns them to the neighborhood, and turns them loose, and the Indians have to get them back as best they can.

At times, the Indians become desperate, and form in mobs to resist these depredations. Then immediately word is sent to the authorities, that the Indians have risen in rebellion; and a company of armed soldiers is sent to the landowner, who, with the soldiers, hunts the Indians like wild beasts, and shoots them down in cold blood.

Those directly responsible for this terrible condition are the priests, who have had the Indians in hand ever since the Spanish conquest. They have posed as the Indians' friends and advisers though all the while betraying them. They have always opposed any plan to help elevate them, and have kept them in ignorance and superstition. Drunkenness has been encouraged by these priests. In fact, the use of alcohol is always a complement to their religious feasts. These feasts are held in each district on an average of about every two months, the priests send-

Llamas Carrying Grain over the Mountains

ing out messengers to announce them and summon the people to come. The Indians are made to understand that these feasts are in honor of Christ, and every means is used to persuade and compel them to attend. Those who are disinclined to do so are many times threatened with fine and imprisonment.

On the day designated, the Indians gather by the thousands in the village of the district. Many large cans of alcohol are placed in conspicuous places, and large quantities are sold to the Indians. Costumes and masks of the most hideous design are also sold to them, some of these representing animals, and some the devil. After a few hours, both men and women become very drunk. Even the children drink. Then the priests organize a procession. A large image of Christ or of one of the saints is brought out of the church building. This image is placed on a platform, and carried on the shoulders of four men. Smaller images are delivered to others of the crowd; and the priest, leading the procession, marches with the people solemnly around the church building to the Indian music. In many instances, the Indians carrying these images are so drunk they are hardly able to walk.

The priest, after leading the procession around for about half an hour, again enters the church building, the crowd following, and the images are deposited in the front part of the church. The priest then immediately be-

A MASK USED BY INDIAN DANCERS

gins to say mass, all the people meanwhile being prostrated in front of the image, on the church floor. The Indians bring their offerings to the priests, and go out again to take part in the revelry.

When these Indians become intoxicated, they are very savage, and fight among themselves. Many are wounded, some are killed. The cursing is terrible to hear. The intoxicated Indian women, when dancing, not infrequently fall upon their babes, which they carry in shawls on their backs. The babes are thus seriously hurt, and sometimes killed outright.

It is a fearful sight to see the hundreds, yes, thousands of drunken, dancing, fighting people, their hair hanging over their faces. Many are covered with blood. Those who are too drunk to seek shelter lie out on the cold plains all night, and many of these die from exposure. Some are killed in the bullfights that take place during the latter part of the feast.

These bullfights are carried on in this way: In the main plaza of the village, the streets are blocked up; and into the inclosure thus formed, the bulls are led, after having been

Teaching Children to Dance and Drink Alcohol

tormented until they are furious. Then many of the drunken Indians are persuaded to enter the inclosure with the furious animals, to "show off." As they run about, teasing the bulls with their shawls, and striking them, many Indians are seriously wounded, being gored and trodden underfoot, and some are killed. During all this time, the priest can be seen mingling with the people, rubbing his hands together in evident satisfaction.

These feasts continue for days. After the Indians' money is all gone, they return to their huts. They are in a most pitiful condition, their clothes dirty and torn, their faces wild and haggard; and many never return. Wives are wailing for their husbands. Little children are weeping bitterly because their fathers have been killed; and in some cases, both father and mother have died during the feast. Many young Indian girls have been ruined and infected with horrible diseases by the hoodlums of the villages. And all this in the name of Jesus!

It is through these religious feasts that drunkenness has become universal among the Indians. In fact, the drinking of alcohol is regarded by them as a virtue. The priests encourage also the chewing of coca leaves, from which cocaine is extracted. This distorts their faces, pollutes their breath, deadens their nerves, and dulls their mental faculties, robbing them of every vestige of intelligence. These vicious habits have degraded the Indians to the extreme, undermined their naturally strong constitutions, and brought upon them much disease. Smallpox, typhoid fever, dysentery, and many other diseases are prevalent among them.

Christ has been entirely misrepresented to them by the priests. The Indians regard Him as a strange, mystic being who cannot be touched by pity, and who loves only the priests; and they are taught that any favors they are to receive from Him must come through the priests. This accounts for the abject obedience they render to the priests, and the priests have taken advantage of this to enrich themselves and satisfy their own lusts.

CHAPTER VII

A Transformation

THIS was the condition when we located among the Indians at Plateria. Chief Camacho let us have part of his house to live in; and it was here that the mission was started. Like wildfire the news spread that the missionary had come to help them and care for them in their sickness.

The Indians have no idea of how to treat their sick, but they have many superstitious ideas about treatments. For sprains and fractures, they kill snakes, cut them open, and tie them around the injured part. Over a wound or a bruise, they sometimes bind leaves; at other times, a piece of sheep's liver. These exclude the air, and cause infection. In pneumonia cases, some will kill a black cat, cut it open, and while it is still warm, tie it on the chest. In cases of insanity — which fortunately are very rare — they beat the patient all over the body with a prickly plant that imparts a terrible burning sensation.

Hundreds came to us for treatment. We were busy from early morning till late at night. Many of the sick had to be carried to

The First Mission Headquarters

us in blankets, and we fitted up a small room in which to house some of the worst cases. Many were in a pitiable condition, covered with vermin and filth, and with scabs under which the pus was visible.

We ministered personally to all that we possibly could; but they came in such numbers that we were obliged to enlist the help of the Indians themselves.

One of the first things we taught the Indians was how to keep clean. We organized several washing classes, with fifteen to twenty persons in each class, providing basins and towels and soap for them, and taught them how to wash themselves. It was pitiful, and sometimes amusing, to see them. They would scrub one part of the face until we told them to move on for fear they would rub the skin off. But in a comparatively short time, they learned. They were enthusiastic, and enjoyed being clean. Sometimes people from the villages near would come and visit us, and would sneer at us, and say, "Did we not tell you that these Indians were worse than the beasts, not knowing enough even to wash themselves?" The only answer we would give was to ask these critics what condition they would be in, and what condition we would be in, if we had not had good mothers or some one else to teach us.

While we were treating the Indians, we prayed with them, and told them of the love of Jesus and the plan of salvation; and as we explained these things, the Indians would almost invariably exclaim: "Oh, we did not know that before! We did not know that Jesus loved us. We did not know that it was wrong to drink alcohol or to use cocaine."

In one of our first meetings for the Indians, a young man of gigantic stature, who had become a wreck through using cocaine and drinking alcohol, came out from the crowd, and taking me by the arm, looked me earnestly in the face, and asked fervently, "Do you mean to tell me that Jesus loves me?"

I answered, "Yes, my son, He does."

"Oh," he said, "tell me again, do you really mean to say that Jesus loves me?"

Tears were streaming down his rough face. It seemed almost too much for him to comprehend, after the life that he had led.

God blessed in a marvelous manner from the very first. People who were carried to us in blankets, were able, after a few days of treatments, to walk away fully restored to health.

During the services, many of the Indians would at once take the cocaine leaves out of their mouths, and throw them away. Soon a wonderful difference was noted in the people of that neighborhood. They were clean, and drunkenness ceased almost wholly among them.

The Indians of more remote regions soon began to call for us to come and visit them. We had no saddle animals at that time, but the Indians would provide horses for us. On one of these occasions, I borrowed Chief Camacho's horse; and while I was taking care of some sick in the village, the horse was stolen from the inclosure. I sent out some Indian friends in different directions to try to find it, I myself taking the main highway.

After I had gone about a mile, on looking back, I saw a man coming toward me on horseback; and as he came near me, I saw that he was mounted upon my borrowed horse.

I tried to appear unconcerned, and walked toward the man at a leisurely pace, hoping to get near enough to grasp the horse's bridle.

When the man was within about fifty feet of me, he suddenly wheeled the horse, at the same time spurring him vigorously, and galloped off at furious speed toward the mountains on the other side of the village.

As I was returning to the village, I thought of the borrowed ax head that was lost, as recorded in 2 Kings 6:5-7; and I felt that if God would take an interest in a borrowed ax head, He would also have an interest in my borrowed horse.

When I reached the house where I was stopping in the village, I told my host about the stolen horse. "Your horse is here," he said. "A few moments ago, a little boy came leading the horse, saying that a man had asked him to deliver it at this house."

When we arrived at the distant places to which we had been called, we would find the people gathered by hundreds with their sick to be treated. Whole provinces were down with smallpox and typhoid fever.

At the same time that we were caring for the people, we carried on an educational campaign among them, teaching them how to keep well. We vaccinated many, thus staying the spread of smallpox.

In some districts, the springs were the main cause of typhoid epidemics, the custom being for many of the people to come to one spring and dip into it their dirty jugs and jars, thus polluting the water. In one of the first places where we found typhoid, we investigated the spring. It was covered with a dirty scum; and after removing this, we dug out 364 toads that had made their home there. We cleaned the spring out, and curbed it with stones, putting in a small galvanized iron pipe, from which the people could get water without dipping in their jugs and jars. For years, there has not been a case of typhoid fever in that district.

We also taught the Indians how to take care of their sick, how to eliminate the vermin that infested their homes, and how to give simple treatments, like fomentations and compresses, in fever cases. We found that cleanliness, with plenty of pure water to drink, and the simplest treatments, worked marvels.

Many times, the people did not wholly follow our instructions in reference to drinking pure water and using the simple compresses and fomentations, because it was difficult for

INDIAN WATER CARRIER

them to believe that clear water would be a help to them. So we would leave with them a coloring matter to put into the water; and after that, they would follow directions implicitly, applying the compresses as instructed.

The most terrible cases were those of smallpox, and it was usually black smallpox that these Indians had. Often we were called too late. But we would apply the cooling compresses, and relieve the breathing by cleansing their throats from the bloody mucus and pus that had gathered, and through our interpreter, we would explain the loving-kindness of Jesus, and the plan of salvation, and pray for them and with them. Faces that had been drawn with pain and fear of death a moment before would take on a peaceful look; and in many instances, a happy smile would spread over them as by faith the saving power of Jesus was grasped. I believe that many of these poor Indians were saved in their very last moments because God took into account that they had had no other opportunity.

There was once brought to me a boy only twelve years old whose sight had been destroyed by smallpox some years before, the disease having eaten away the very eyeballs.

Indian 110 Years Old, from Whom the First Mission Land Was Purchased

The little fellow was crying bitterly, and was exclaiming pitifully, *"Chamaccowa,"* meaning that everything seemed dark to him. I gathered the boy in my arms, holding my face close beside his, and explained to him that Jesus knew all about him, and that he should not grieve so. I told him that God would restore his sight in heaven, and that he would see beautiful things, far surpassing anything on this earth. The little fellow stopped crying, and asked many intelligent questions; and I left him happy in his new-found faith.

The following from a correspondent to the Puna *La Union* of March 10, 1913, indicates how some of the people in the vicinity of Plateria regarded the work of our mission there:

"THE INDIANS AND THE PROTESTANTS

"Juli, January 20, 1913.

"Sir Director:

"The Protestants among the Aymaras of these regions do not mix with politics; they concern themselves with making good men, civilizing them.

A TRANSFORMATION

"They are not thinking of how they may combat the government or get control of it; their mission is holier, nobler, and better.

"The paper published here tells better than we can, the facts gathered during a visit the editors have just made to the Indians.

"We are sending the clipping in question, as correspondents of your weekly paper. It says:

"Having a great desire to find means of bettering the condition of the Indian, we wished to become informed of the results obtained by those employed by the Protestants; and with this purpose, we went to La Plateria, which is located on a hill on the highway from Acora to Puno, well populated, and pleasing in appearance. On either side of the road are two buildings with galvanized roofs, which by their dimensions, symmetry in the location of doors and windows, in a word, by their structure, clearly show that those who planned them were something more than Indians, and something more than owners of country villas. We presented ourselves at one of these places, and there came out to receive us an Indian woman of some thirty-five or forty years, with a baby in her arms. We asked for the Yankee brethren, and she told us that they were absent. She invited us into a room where she and her husband lived. Within the room were Bible pictures and reading textbooks, arranged on a little table, together with a slate pencil and writing materials, rare things to find in the house of an Indian.

"With the greatest naturalness, frankness, and friendliness,— things almost never met in those of her race,— the Indian woman told us of the progress that had been made, showing us photographs of brethren who in increasing numbers had been baptized, and of the number of marriages celebrated among them. In short, it was a dialogue in the Aymara language, which we transfer to these columns as accurately as possible.

"'And how do you differ from the other Indians of the villages if you continue following the same customs as they?' we asked.

"'In much,' she answered. 'We never drink alcohol nor maize beer, neither do we chew coca leaves, things so harmful for the body and the soul that it is enough that you see these pictures to convince yourselves,' whereat she showed us some terrible figures, where were represented in colors the ravages of alcohol on the human organism, in the family, and in society. And she told us about cocaine, the poison that is extracted from the coca leaves.

"'And then in the festivities of the people, on the days of rejoicing, and above all, at

AYMARA INDIAN HAIR DRESSING

marriages and funerals, how do you manage it with those who attend that are not brethren?'

"'Very simply, in two ways,' she replied. 'First, we do not have feasts in honor of the saints, nor wakes nor devotions where so much is drunk and so many crimes and sins are committed; and secondly, because we separate ourselves completely from the rest of the villagers, and at marriages, and above all, at funerals, where they drink so much that they even profane the corpses and commit indecencies over the tomb, we only drink tea made of sage or of the camomile, and serve bread to those who have come.'

"Thus she continued telling us how, after cleansing of the soul, there should follow cleansing of the body, in fulfillment of which they wash themselves daily, and twice a week wash their clothes. In truth, both she and her child were in such a state of cleanliness that no spot could be found. Going on, she told us of the school of Brother Camacho, where she had learned to read, and where even the elderly people attended and learned. Her conversation was such that it was a real pleasure to hear her speak.

"At this point, an Indian brother arrived, who happily surprised us by the cleanness of his clothes and the whiteness of his teeth, in a mouth with a perfect smile, and

Indian Convert Plowing with a Crooked Stick

without those dark green tints which make the mouth of every coca chewer so loathsome.

"With him we carried on a similar conversation on the same topics.

"Our new arrival enthusiastically sang several songs in a very acceptable voice. We were about to leave, but the Indian offered us lodging, which we could not accept, because we would have to hurry on; and then he spoke to us of charity in this way:

"'In this world, nothing is ours. No one can say absolutely that this or that is mine; no, because all things earthly were made by God, for His children, mankind, who are equal, of course, even though the color of their skin be different. Therefore we offer our bread to the traveler, and share our milk with the wayfarer. With this purpose in view, we are going to build an inn in which to lodge travelers, as we now have a hospital and medicines for all.'

"'They tell us,' we said, 'that you do not obey the authorities, and hate the landlords.'

"'It is false,' he responded. 'Jesus said, To Cæsar what is Cæsar's, but to God what is God's. So it is that we obey the authorities, for they also were recognized by the Master, for the order and good of communities. We do not hate the landlords, nor do we covet their property as others, for by our work we get all we need; and as God does not forget to give daily food to the birds of the fields, neither will He forget us who are His children.'

"It would be a long story to tell all that we talked about with them, and for the present it is sufficient that we make known that such is the transformation of the Indian, that we admire the consecration and energy the missionaries of La Plateria have known how to use so liberally, in converting the Indian from a dirty, drunken, insincere, lazy, and savage being into one endowed with his right mind, temperate, a worker, and with such good sentiments that we can do no less than send to Mr. Stahl, head of the mission, our most sincere congratulations, and offer him the modest aid of our paper in favor of the great work that has been planned, and whose beneficent results we have been privileged to witness personally, only regretting that we did not have the opportunity of meeting him, to greet him, to gather better data, and more fully to appreciate the uses for which the large buildings are designed that have been constructed by them for the benefit of our downtrodden aboriginal race, which later will be another race, if such apostles as these continue the great work begun with the faith of those who doubt nothing when they place at the service of helpless humanity their lives and energies.—*From 'Integridad.'*"

CHAPTER VIII

By Way of Encouragement

ONE day, as my wife and I were busy treating the many sick who came to us at the little hut where we were then living, a messenger appeared, asking us to go and care for the daughter of a chief who lived up on the mountains. This was about ten o'clock in the morning; and because of numerous grave cases that came to us that day, I was not able to get away until seven o'clock that evening. By the time my Indian guide and I reached the mountain top, I could not see my hand before my face. I noticed that the guide, instead of taking the

THE SICK COMING TO THE PLATERIA DISPENSARY

lead, as he had done formerly, was lagging behind; and I asked him why he did so. He answered that he had lost the way. Breathing a prayer for guidance, I took the lead in the direction that I thought the chief's messenger had given us. As I was hurrying along over the rough ground, urging my horse ahead, suddenly there was a vivid flash of lightning, revealing my horse's feet within six inches of the brink of a terrible precipice. Another instant and I would have been dashed down to the rocks hundreds of feet below. I quickly drew my horse back and dismounted, thanking God for delivering me. This was the only flash of lightning that evening; and I believe that God let His light shine over my path to guide my footsteps.

We made our way carefully down the other side of the mountain, and the barking of dogs soon revealed that we were approaching the huts of some Indians. This proved to be where the chief lived. We passed the night at his house, returning to the mission the following morning.

We had to do considerable minor surgery, and the confidence the Indians put in us was really wonderful. They thought we were able to do almost everything. Many a one has come to us, telling us that he had pains in his chest, and asking if we would not please cut out his lungs and heart. At other times, some would ask for memory medicine, or for medicine to make them good.

The Indians will stand any amount of pain if they are treated kindly. Many times, away out in the mountains, our supply of anæsthetics has run out, and we have had to perform minor operations without any.

There once came to us a chief from a distant region, who had had his middle finger torn off, it having become entangled in a rope attached to an ox that became frightened. In his crude way, he had tried to cure the finger by tying over it a piece of sheep's liver. When he came to us, over a month afterward, his hand had become badly infected through the decaying liver. We had no anæsthetic on hand at that time; and I explained to the man what would have to be done in order to save his hand, if not his life. I told him that it was going to hurt, but that we would not hurt him any more than was positively necessary. While talking to him, I put my arm around him; and when I had

Our First Mission House Going Up at Plateria

finished explaining to him, he put out his injured hand to me, and said, "Father, you can go right ahead and do what you think is best." Then, taking from his head a woolen cap such as the Indians in that region always wear, he crowded it into his mouth as far as possible. I asked my interpreter what the man meant by this. "Oh," he said, "he is stuffing his mouth full so that he will not cry out and will have something to bite on!" I removed the finger at the last joint, cut away the putrid flesh, applied the antiseptics, and bandaged the stump. The man never flinched.

Hundreds of the Indians come to us with aching teeth. We never took any training in dentistry in the States, and did not even know how to pull a tooth. But we sent for some forceps, and as soon as they came, we proceeded to use them.

The Indians are great missionaries themselves. As they travel about from place to place, they are always telling others about the gospel; and not a Sabbath passes but some bring strangers to church. Sometimes an Indian will have hold of the hands of two other Indians, half leading them and half dragging them to the front part of the church. Then he will say, "Pastor, here are two new brothers." We go down to these new people, who are so bashful, and shake hands with them, and make them feel at home. This has helped materially to bring up the work.

Soon our Sabbath attendance reached an average of six hundred persons; and erelong many of them were baptized, and we had the privilege of organizing a church. We held our Sabbath meetings out of doors at that time, not having any church building.

In our work for the Indians, we have not carried the idea that to be a Christian is to have a long face, and not have legitimate enjoyment. We call the Indians in our districts together every two or three months for a day of diversion and sociability. On these occasions, they bring their lunches with them, and make a day of it.

We have introduced different athletic games, and the Indians are much interested in these. Football, while not carried on "according to Hoyle," has been a source of great enjoyment to them. We have swings for the children, and foot races and tests of strength for the men.

At one time, thinking to have a tug of war, I called for a large, strong rope, and the Indians brought me one of thick leather. I explained the game to them, drawing a line across the yard, and placed twenty young men on each end of the rope. They pulled most vigorously; and the spectators became so excited that they forgot themselves so far as to take sides with their friends, until there were about a hundred on each side. Mothers, daughters, and sweethearts took part. As all were laughing and pulling enthusiastically, the rope parted in the middle, and a greater scrambling you never saw.

The Indians are very fond of music; and after we had been among them about a year, the young men asked us to send to the United States for some band instruments for them. We did so, and soon we had a large band fitted out with cornets, clarinets, bass horns, and cymbals. I can tell you there is not another band in all the world that can beat it for noise.

We found the Indians an intellectual people, notwithstanding the general belief that they were stupid. Their stupidity went only as far as their vices went. As soon as they

BY WAY OF ENCOURAGEMENT 151

left off these vices, and were healed of their diseases, they were as capable a people as could be found anywhere in the world.

They have good reasoning powers. The following case will illustrate this fact:

OUR FIRST CHOIR AMONG THE INDIANS

While one of our Sabbath meetings was in progress, a priest rode up, and dismounting, took a seat among the people. As he listened, he became very nervous. The lesson was on true Sabbath observance, being an explanation of the fourth commandment. After the priest had listened for a few minutes, he suddenly rose, and said in a loud voice, in the

Indian language: "This is all false. The seventh-day Sabbath is an old institution, and was done away long ago. It does not serve us any more. It is too old."

As he stopped a moment for breath, one of the Indians arose in the audience, and said, "Mr. Priest, you say that the Sabbath is too old, that it does not serve us any more?"

"Yes, I did," yelled the priest.

"Well, now, Mr. Priest," the Indian continued, "the sun, the moon, and the stars are old; but God made them, and they still serve us. Why should the Sabbath not serve us, too, even though it is old? God made that, didn't He?"

The priest did not answer a word, but immediately mounted his horse and rode off, and has never since been seen in that district.

In their natural sphere, the Indians are far ahead of the white men. They are able to trace a thief for miles over the rough mountains; and if a footprint shows plainly in the dust, they can determine with ease to whom the foot belongs. They can tell the exact time by the sun, and they know weather conditions perfectly. On one occasion, as we

A Group of Straw Boats on Lake Titicaca

were starting out in our boat to visit some of the Indians who lived on the little peninsula extending into Lake Titicaca, an old Indian standing near warned us not to go, telling us that in a few hours the lake would be very rough. We could not understand why he should say this, because we saw no indication of coming storm. We questioned him, and he asked, "Don't you see the way those clouds are hanging?" He tried, in his simple way, to explain to us; but we did not believe him, and started on our voyage. In a few hours, we had reason to regret our decision; for the waves ran so high that our boat capsized, and we were nearly drowned.

These Indians are generous and noble-hearted. One day when I had made a trip into the mountains to visit some sick people, night overtook me before I could return to the mission. I asked permission from some Indians who lived on the mountain to pass the night in their hut. They gave me a place to sleep; but as soon as I lay down, I began to cough. The woman of the house brought a large blanket, and covered me carefully; still I continued to cough. In a few moments, she brought in another blanket, and put that also over me. I coughed again, and she added a third blanket. As these blankets were made of llama wool, they were very heavy, weighing from ten to twelve pounds each. I could not keep from coughing; and the woman brought a blanket every time I coughed, until she had put nine blankets over me.

At another time, I was out on the plains with my two Indian guides, expecting to be able to return to some friends before nightfall; but night overtook us, and it was very dark, and we had to stop. We were not prepared to spend the night out; but we took the few saddle pads we had, and spread them on the ground, and I lay down with a guide on each side of me. They explained that I should lie in the middle so that they could protect me from the cold. After about half an hour, I heard whisperings between the two guides, and wondered what it signified. They evidently thought I was fast asleep. Then they took off their outer clothing, and covered me with it. They were content and happy to suffer the cold all night in order to do me this kindness.

156 IN THE LAND OF THE INCAS

The Indians have superior business ethics also. For some time after I arrived here, I had to buy certain supplies from them, such as standing barley for the horses. Many a time, as I suggested a price for the produce, the owner would say, "No, brother, that is too much; pay me so much," naming an amount far less than I had offered to him.

CHAPTER IX

"Christianity" That Is Not Christian

AFTER we had been three or four months in this region, the Roman Catholic priests commenced fierce and systematic persecution against us and the Indians. These priests would announce their feasts, and send out their messengers to demand the presence of the people, as they had done formerly; but as the Indians had given up the use of alcohol, they did not choose to go to the feasts. Where there had been formerly an attendance of several thousands, soon there were not even a hundred present. Though not all the Indians at once accepted the gospel, they did cease to permit the priests to deceive them. The priests went from house to house personally, pleading with the people, begging them to attend the feasts; and when they would not go, the priests threatened and even beat many of them.

There was no religious liberty in Peru in those days, not even tolerance of other than the state religion. We were regarded as lawbreakers. We were insulted on every hand; stones were thrown at us; and when we went through the villages, often the streets were blocked by the people, and as we passed by, our horses were struck with clubs, and we were threatened with death. Our Indian brethren were in some instances beaten almost to death. At one time, a priest and three other men went to the house of one of the Indians who would not attend the feasts, and threatened him with death, in an attempt to make him promise that he would attend the next feast. But this man, Juan Huanca by name, refused to promise, saying that he did not drink alcohol any more. At this, the priests began to kick him, and picking up a large club, struck him several times across the chest with it, and left him lying on the ground for dead. The Indian's only answer was, "You can kill the body, but you can't kill the soul," and he would not promise. For months, he lay between life and death. I attended him, and am glad to say that eventually he recovered. This is but one of the many hundreds of such instances.

The Indians many times were severely misused by the saloon keepers and their colleagues. As one of our Indian teachers was going through a village, he was taken forcibly

DARITEO, ONE OF OUR INDIAN TEACHERS

(159)

into a saloon by three men, who tried to compel him to drink a glass of liquor. While two of the men held him, the third placed the glass to his lips. But the Indian succeeded in freeing one of his hands; and in defending himself, he dashed the glass into the man's own face. Instead of being angry, the man immediately told the others to release the Indian, and commended him for his resistance.

One of the Indians who had given up the alcohol habit, was working for one of the large landowners near the mission. One evening, three men seized him, threw him to the ground, pried his mouth open with a stick, and poured a bottle of alcohol down his throat. He became intoxicated, and was ill as a result of his rough treatment.

As I was going through a large village, the people on the streets called after me in the Indian language, of which at that time I did not understand much. My little son, who was with me, understood the language, and spoke it readily. As we proceeded down the street, the people continued to call after us. I supposed that they were greeting me, and I nodded my head from side to side to them, and answered, *"Who-mar-es-ca-ma-ki,"* which is the usual response to a greeting, and means, "The same to you."

After we reached the other end of the village, my son asked, "Papa, do you know what those people were calling after you?"

I answered, "No, my son, I do not."

"Why," he said, "they were calling you devil, and all manner of bad things, and said you had horns; and you said, 'The same to you.'"

No one molested me when I returned to that village. Somehow I was reminded of a text in the fifth of Matthew, which says, "Agree with thine adversary quickly."

Every day, there came to us messages warning us that we were going to be killed. About this time, we bought from one of the Indians a small piece of land upon which to erect some very necessary mission buildings — a small hospital, a school building, and a dwelling house. As soon as we started to put the buildings up, the priest became very active to hinder the work in every way. Word was sent out that any one who would work on these buildings was to be arrested, and that if we did not desist at once, we would be killed. But we kept right on working. I cannot say that these evil reports, coming, as they did, every day, had no effect upon us. At times, we felt decidedly apprehensive, especially upon the feast days, when large crowds from the village would gather where we were building, and curse and throw stones at our people. At first, our people wanted to retaliate; but we explained to them that these poor souls knew not what they were doing, and that we were to remember what our dear Saviour passed through for our sakes, and should work on quietly, and when stones were thrown, seek shelter as best we could. This they did.

Shortly after this, the bishop of Puno, named Ampuero, with a mob of two hundred men, all on horseback, came out to the mission. It so happened that Mrs. Stahl and I were not there at the time, having gone to buy some supplies. The first thing the bishop did was to take the keys away from our caretaker, and appropriate some things, and break up others.

Then the mob tried to compel the Indians living about the mission to kneel before the bishop and kiss his hand. This they refused to do, however; whereupon the bishop became

"CHRISTIANITY" NOT CHRISTIAN

enraged, and told the people to bind the Indians with stout leather cords and make prisoners of them. Six of our Indian brethren were bound arm to arm, and driven, hatless and coatless, to Puno, twenty-one miles distant. On the way, the mob beat them, and tried to ride over them with their horses. At Puno, the Indians were thrown into jail.—

As soon as we received notice of the affair, we immediately went to Puno, taking food to our Indian brethren who were in jail, and otherwise attending to their needs. Then we called upon the most prominent people of the city in their behalf. The bishop accused these Indians of having assaulted him with clubs. We visited the judges, and other officials of the court, explaining to them that these Indians did not drink alcohol any more, and that they were accused falsely by the bishop.

As the last day of the trial approached, and the judge was to give his final verdict, I went to see him, explaining to him the work that had been done for the Indians, and told him courteously that some day he would be called before the great judgment seat of God, and would have to answer for the judgment rendered upon these poor, misused people. He seemed to be impressed, and told me, as I left him, that he would judge the imprisoned Indians justly. And he did; for that afternoon, he released them from prison.

The Puno *La Union* thus reports this experience of the Indians, and comments upon it, in its issue of March 10, 1913:

"THE IMPRISONMENT OF THE PROTESTANTS

"On learning that the Protestant natives from La Plateria had been brought from Chucuito to the police station of this city, we went to interview the subprefect of the Cercado to gather data as to their imprisonment.

"The subprefect informed us that these natives had failed to recognize the fact that the very illustrious bishop was a prelate, and neither had they recognized the political authorities.

"On inquiry, on our part, if there was some definite act revealing such lack of recognition, he replied that we should speak with his lordship the prefect, which we said we would not do, for various reasons. Then he told us he had asked for a report from his

INDIANS AND SHRINE BEFORE A CHURCH NEAR CUZCO

very illustrious majesty the bishop, and that when he went to Chucuito with public authority, he found that these natives had been made prisoners.

"Afterward, we went to the police station to interview these unhappy Indians, and from them we obtained the following version:

"'I,' said Camacho, 'taking a bottle of salts, went with this remedy to see one of our sick brethren, when his very illustrious majesty the bishop arrived at my house with two hundred individuals on foot and mounted, finding there only my son of eleven years, who told him that I had left the house.' At once they carried the son away a prisoner, first, however, entering Mr. Stahl's house, gathering more prisoners, whom they asked the reason why they no longer cared to observe the religious feasts, etc.

"As soon as Camacho heard of the invasion of the district, he hastened to interview the illustrious bishop, who refused to answer or greet him. Immediately made a prisoner, he was taken with the rest to the prison in Chucuito, where they were allowed no food, being brought afterward to this town as best they could be.

"CHRISTIANITY" NOT CHRISTIAN 167

"We hope to get the official facts that may shed more light on this extraordinary happening.

"Just in these moments we are informed that the arrested natives have been transferred to the public prison.

"WILL THERE BE JUSTICE?

"The detained natives are still in jail!

"What is happening is unheard-of!

"A proof that the authorities here are a danger and never a protection, is the fact that the Protestant natives, victims of religious persecution, are still imprisoned, locked up by the unconscionable action of the conscienceless authorities.

"If the judiciary do not manifest themselves just and inflexible this time, granting guaranties to some Indians who are apostles of the regeneration of their race, we will have to turn nihilists, that is, proclaim the abolition of all authority.

"But fortunately we have here men of strength who are disposed to defend our liberties with the holy lash of strong words, and capable of lambasting the despots who make of public authority their paper armor.

"We are not alone. The honorable press, which is the exponent of the culture we have gained in Peru, will know how to fulfill its mission in the face of such enormous abuses of right, liberty, and the culture of our land.

"Judges, if you know how to judge, give proof of it, by administering on this occasion a quick, prompt, and impartial justice, that there may not fall on you and yours the curse of the victims and their children.

"Are you fathers of families? So are they also.

"It is not now the arbitrary imprisonment into which citizens were thrown in Huancané, through the action of military judgment which proved itself unlawful.

"Neither is it the assassinations which the governor of Inchupalla perpetrated with his now fugitive band.

"It is something more, which is happening in another center, nearer this capital of the department, in which its highest political and ecclesiastical authorities, by mutual agreement, are following the forbidden road of iniquitous vandalism.

"It is known that in the section of La Plateria, six leagues from this capital, the al-

"CHRISTIANITY" NOT CHRISTIAN

truism of a Yankee has established a center of evangelical propaganda with such results that in three years of beneficent labor, the Indian has been made a useful being, free from the vices that so much characterize his race.

"The evangelized Indian does not drink alcohol, he does not chew coca leaves, he is clean, he is moral; and now he can read, he

THE FIRST BAPTISM AMONG THE INDIANS

has acquired habits of order and a desire to work, or he is sociable and exercises charity. They have a large ranch, a school, a hospital, and an inn for lodging.

"This highly beneficial work for the regeneration of the Indian, which receives favorable notice even in distant sections, has been menaced by the diocesan zeal of Bishop Monseñor Ampuero, who in person, and accompanied by some poor devils from the town of Chucuito, in an infernal cavalcade like the hosts of a new Attila, set out to pursue the Indians; let it not be thought to persuade them by word or example—no; but to hale them to prison after maltreating them. They were bound, and then taken to the jail in Chucuito, whence the subprefect of the prison ordered them brought under guard to this capital, lodging them in the police station. The very illustrious bishop returned to the interior of the peninsula, bent on the same kind of mission.

"Following this extraordinary procedure, a general indignation has arisen, even among members of the police force.

"Where are we?

"Does his lordship the prefect believe that such affronts may be made against individual liberty, human dignity, and the Bill of Rights?

"*La Union* will not be the only organ of the press that condemns such reprehensible acts. The whole press of the republic will follow, when the enormity of the facts is known.

"What crime is it to be a 'Protestant,' that is, to enjoy the natural liberty of conscience?

"Is it a social evil, this work of dignifying the race and lifting it to the station of a man who is conscientious and useful to society?

"God forbid!

"The progressive towns, such as Puno, if they recognize it well, have that which authorizes them to protest, in the name of morality and the laws, against the way the prefect Torres Angulo has favored the very illustrious bishop Monseñor Ampuero in the unlawful and barbaric acts of which we are speaking.

"It is apparent that this department, without local government, because of the hastily provided principal and other authorities, needs to petition the government now directing the destinies of the country that officials be sent here who are acquainted with the local needs and are well informed of the spirit of the laws. Ignorance is a danger in the matter of administration."

A LETTER WRITTEN BY CAMACHO
"Puno Prison, March 7, 1913.
"Señor Doctor Don Isaac Deza,
"City.
"Esteemed Doctor:
"May peace and health be yours in the bosom of your estimable family.

"I am in this prison separated from my tender children, who have lost their mother, and I do not know how they are faring.

"I entreat you to act as lawyer for those of us who have been thrown into prison by Bishop Don Valentín Ampuero, who, accompanied by the governor and two justices of the peace from Chucuito, came to that place with that object.

"The circumstances were as follows:

"The third of this month, Bishop Don Valentín Ampuero, accompanied by Governor Don José Sotomayor and two justices of the peace of Chucuito, with more than two hundred men from among the residents of said town and the Indians from various ranches,

Indian Families Returning from Market, Puno, Peru

broke into my home, where they found only my young children, since I had left the house. Believing that I had hidden myself, they broke down the doors; but not finding me, they carried my minor son, Patricio, away a prisoner. After breaking into the homes of other native Protestants, they turned to the house of Mr. Stahl, where they found the servant Jacinto Tarqui, from whom they secured the keys; and opening the rooms, they broke up the furniture. Then they called out of their houses other natives, to ask them where the Yankee was, and at once told them that all who were not of the gospel belief should go to one side, and that the believers should be seized, which was done with the eight of us who are here imprisoned. As soon as I presented myself before the bishop, he called me a heretic, and ordered that I also should be seized, the eight of us being brought in such harassed condition to the jail in Chucuito, whence we were conducted to this city by a force of gendarmes sent for the purpose.

"I inclose a list of the residents who accompanied the bishop.

"Respectfully yours,
"M. Z. Camacho."

Peru is a Catholic state, and Roman Catholicism is the state religion. Up to November, 1915, the constitution of Peru made it possible to banish from the country for three years any one who held religious services other than Catholic. In the larger cities near the coast, the law has been rarely appealed to; but in the interior, and especially where Protestant missionaries have been helping to lift the Indians to a higher life, the priests and the landlords and the zealots have been stirred as they have seen their hold upon the Indians slipping, and the consequent loss of reverence. But the attitude of the priests toward this work has roused a sense of justice and equality and sympathy for the Indians in good men, who have protested against the intolerance of the priesthood. The following document is an indication of the growth of this sentiment; it speaks for itself.

"SUPREME GOVERNMENT DECREE

"Lima, September 2, 1914.

"After having reviewed the attached record of the cause pursued by virtue of the petition presented by the secretary of the Pro-Indigena Association, complaining of the abuse of which the aborigine Claudio de la Cruz has been the victim, from whom it is attempted to exact payment of a fine because he refused to discharge gratis the burden of steward of a certain religious feast due to be celebrated in the village of Otao, province of Huarochiri; and—

"*Whereas,* It is a primordial guarantee recognized in the constitution of the state, article 14, that no one is obliged to do that which the law does not demand, nor prohibited from doing that which the law does not forbid; and—

"*Whereas,* In violation of this fundamental precept, an attempt has been made to compel the Indian, De la Cruz, to furnish, out of his own private property, the expenses of a religious festivity, and for his having resisted this imposition, the trustee of the community, the constable, and the police judge have imposed on him a fine of eighty soles ($38.93 U. S.), with the threat of exclusion from the village commons in case of default; and—

"*Whereas,* The intervention in these matters by the aforementioned public authorities amounts to the misdemeanor of 'exaction' penalized by the law of October 21, 1897, as provided in article 202 of the penal code; and —

"*Whereas,* It is therefore the duty of the government to put an end to this state of things, liberating the Indian race from these antiquated practices which oblige them to bear unjustifiable expenses;

"In harmony with the decision of the Department of Government and Municipalities, and the report of the attorney-general, it is —

"*Resolved,* 1. That it be declared as a general rule, that the burden of steward of feasts celebrated according to the custom of the Indian villages, is not obligatory;

CATHOLIC CHURCH AT LARAOS WHERE MEETINGS WERE HELD BY OUR MISSIONARIES

"2. That all public authorities of whatever character be absolutely prohibited from any intermeddling in the designation of such stewards or in the performance of this burden; and —

"3. That the prefects of departments be charged with special vigilance concerning such abuses of this nature as may be committed, and with the duty of instituting against those responsible for same, proper criminal process.

"It is ordered that this decree be registered, circulated, published, and filed.

"Rubric of His Excellency (President).
"By Fuchs (Prime Minister)."

Owing to the oppression of the Indians near Lake Titicaca by the Roman Catholic bishop of Puno, contrary to the counsel of some of his coreligionists, a senator from that department introduced a bill into the national Congress so to amend the constitution as to give religious liberty to all denominations. The matter dragged along till November, 1915, when it passed Congress. At the first reading of the bill in the Senate, there were only four dissenting votes, and three of these were from Catholic priests. At the second reading, that church put forth strong efforts to defeat it. After two years of such work, but twelve votes could be mustered in the house against the bill. November 11, it passed and was officially promulgated by Congress. The balconies of the chamber were crowded with women, priests, and boys from the convent schools. The president was besieged with petitions to veto the bill, but he neither signed nor vetoed it. Upon its promulgation, the bill became law. The following is a picture of what occurred when the bill passed the house in November, as given by Dr. William O. Stunt, superintendent of the Peru District of the Methodist Episcopal Church, taken from the *Christian Advocate* (New York) of January 6, 1916:

"When the leader of the reform movement, Señor Quimper, entered, he was greeted by the Roman Catholic women with shouts of 'Renegade!' . . . 'Death to Quimper!' 'Death to the heretics!' 'Death to religious liberty!' 'Traitors!' 'Down with Pilate!' 'He's bought by the Protestants!' 'Away with him!' 'Away with him!'

"A few university students had slipped into the center of the crowd of Roman Catholic women, and so occasionally one heard among the shrill voices of the women the husky shouts of these men in behalf of religious freedom. The president of the deputies had hunted up an excuse to stay at home that day, so the duty of presiding fell on the vice president of the deputies, Dr. Pena Murietta. His arrival called forth a storm of protests; and amid the noise of firecrackers, he was showered with crowns of alfalfa. When the senators arrived in a body, they were greeted with 'Traitors!' 'Death to the representatives!' 'Death to the reformers!' 'Death to liberty!' and when the meeting was finally called to order, the tumult in the galleries was such that the presiding officer had to order that one of the balconies should be emptied.

"In the meantime, the priest Sancho Diaz, the leader of the Roman Catholic forces, and a half dozen others, were drinking tea and beer in the barroom adjoining, in the hope of preventing a quorum; but finally, hearing Dr. Pena Murietta proceed with the business of the day, they rushed in, shouting: 'There is no quorum! There is no quorum!' The other congressmen laughed, and said that it would have been their fault if there were not. And so it happened that the very enemies of the bill were present and helped to swell the quorum that made possible the formal announcement of the law.

"By this time, the noise in the galleries was enormous. Women prayed and yelled at the same time, firecrackers were set off, and more alfalfa crowns were hurled at Dr. Pena Murietta as he arose, and with his bell in one hand (to call for order) and the official document in the other, shouted out, 'The honorable Congress being in session in order to announce formally the reform of article 4 of the constitution, I shall announce it!' Like a tiger Sr. Sancho Diaz sprang from his seat, ran to the table, seized the document, and tore it to pieces.

"Some of the congressmen tried to stop him, but were unable to do so. Dr. Pena Murietta, having ordered the offender to be detained, announced the adjournment of the day's session. (A few moments later the priest formally apologized for tearing up the document.) And so closed one of the most extraordinary sessions of the Peruvian Congress."

Thus the bill became law, and other religions than Roman Catholic are tolerated in Peru. But religious liberty is not mere toleration; it recognizes equal rights. May Peru soon complete the good work she has begun.

As yet, religious persecution among the Indians has not ceased; but the law is having its effect. In sections far away from the capital, where priest and official are interested in keeping the Indians enslaved drunkards, there have been violent uprisings; but God has overruled to save the lives of His people.

CHAPTER X

Help from High Sources

ABOUT this time, public sentiment seemed to change in our favor. Apparently the bishop had gone a step too far, and the people were very much displeased with him. They said that he had no right to make prisoners of these Indians. If they had been guilty of a crime, he should have informed the secular authorities, and it was their duty to make prisoners of the offenders. So the bishop left Puno for several months, until things calmed down somewhat.

While this persecution was going on, the priest and the bishop sent letters to the government officials at the capital of Peru, accusing us of inciting the Indians to rebellion and teaching them to disobey the authorities. As a result of these accusations, the president of Peru sent a commission to investigate our work.

When the commissioners arrived, they went out in the province, visiting the Indians. They asked the Indians what the missionaries taught them; and the Indians, in their simple way, answered that they were taught to obey

God, to have regard for the welfare of their fellow men, obey the authorities in every way, and not to drink alcohol nor use cocaine. The commissioners found that the Indians who had accepted the gospel were far more intelligent and more courteous than the others. Their whole appearance was different from that of the Indians who were still drinking alcohol. Our Indians were clean, their clothes were clean, their faces were happy, and there was a bright look in their eyes. Even at a distance, they could be distinguished from the others.

So the commission returned a very favorable report of the mission work; and when, a few months later, a bill for religious liberty was presented before Congress, as told about in the preceding chapter, it passed, although hotly contested by the priests. I met one of the senators afterward, and he told me personally that our mission work was "the lever used to push the bill through the house."

After a few months' absence, Bishop Ampuero returned to this province; and going one day to the village near the mission, he gathered the people around him in the public square, and cursed the mission, and said he would do everything he could to hinder the work and see that the mission buildings were destroyed and the people killed. Ten days from that date, he became very ill and died suddenly; and two weeks after his death, the two priests that were foremost in the persecution also died. Within two months, five of the worst enemies of our mission work had died.

As I was going along the public highway one day shortly after that, a man on horseback overtook me and began to inquire about the mission, asking me who I was, where I was going, etc. I answered all his questions respectfully. He suddenly wheeled his horse about to face me, and putting out his hand, said, "I am Pablo Corpio, the governor of Chucuito." That was the district where our mission was located. He told me that he had not understood our work, and had done all he could to hinder it, but that now his feelings had changed, and he was our friend. He also informed me that there was a plot on foot in the village of Chucuito to kill Chief Camacho, and that I should not permit him to leave his home under any circumstances.

As we were riding along, he requested the privilege of asking a question that might seem strange to me.

I replied, "Say on."

He then said: "Tell me, how is it that five men,— the bishop, two priests, and two men of our village,— have died within a few months. They were all enemies of you and that mission work."

I answered: "Since you ask, I can only tell you plainly my opinion. I believe that it was nothing more nor less than the hand of God. These men stood in the way of God's work, and He saw that it was necessary to put them out of the way. Nothing can hinder the work of God."

He said, "I believe you."

Some of the priests of this province soon left hastily for distant places.

The second day after this, two men called on Camacho and tried to force him to go from the village, on the pretext that the governor wanted to see him. I was at the chief's house at the time, and I forbade him to accompany the men. They asked what business I had to interfere; so I courteously told them that I understood there was a plot under way to kill him and I would not permit him to go with them.

We now organized a day school. One hundred and fifty names were enrolled the first day. Many of those who came to learn to read and write were over forty years old. When I asked them why they wanted to come to school, they answered, "We want to learn to read the letter that God has left for us." They called the Bible the letter that God had left for them.

About this time, Mr. and Mrs. Rojas, of Argentine, were sent up to help us; and they took this school in charge. The Indians were delighted with their school and teachers.

MRS. STAHL AND HER INDIAN SCHOOL

CHAPTER XI

Reconnoitering

I NOW decided to investigate the conditions in this area around Lake Titicaca. So with one of our Indian converts, Stephen, as a guide, I started out. The first day, we made thirty miles, reaching the province of Juli. I had never seen so large an Indian country as lay near this place. There were Indian huts as far as the eye could see, and close together at that. As I looked upon those thousands of huts, and the Indians that lived in them, a great longing rose in my heart to help these people, and give them the precious gospel of Christ.

We passed the night at the home of a Liberal, a man that was a friend to our work and a friend to the Indians.

The next day, after traveling thirty-five miles, we reached Pumata. We could not find a place to stay overnight, nor could we find feed for our mules. I went to the governor of the town, but he would not take us in. He said he had no room. After I had looked about for some time, a poor Indian told us to come to his home, and he gave us feed for

CHULPA, OR ROYAL MONUMENT, UMAYO, PERU

our saddle animals. This Indian family have since been very friendly to our brethren as they have traveled through this place.

Here was a province of over fifteen thousand Indians, and no one to teach them the right way.

The next night, after another thirty miles, we crossed the line into Bolivia. Here we found an immense feast in progress. When we stopped a few moments, the drunken Indians would bow to us and dance around us. Some of them would kneel in front of us, and offer us of their fire water. They were greatly surprised at our refusal. It seemed pitiable to see these thousands of people in ignorance of the right way. They were feasting, drinking, dancing, and cursing, and all this in the name of religion.

The following day, we reached Tiahuanuco, the city of the old Pre-Inca ruins; and I spent a few hours visiting these monuments of a long forgotten people. I was much impressed with the magnitude of the stones that had been used to build the vast temples at this place. As I saw how great stone idols were cracking and crumbling before the elements,

I was reminded of Psalm 144: 15: "Happy is that people, whose God is the Lord."

We passed through some very thickly populated districts in this region, all in the same condition,— in the depths of idolatry and vice. At every place where we stopped, there was opportunity to treat sick persons. At one of these places, we found a man suffering with a broken leg, and I set it for him. We left him some reading matter, for which he was very thankful.

In a few days, we reached Caraboca, a fine, large Indian village on the shore of the lake. The Indians told us that the governor received travelers, so we went to him. As soon as he learned that I had a knowledge of medicine, he wished me to see a very sick child of his; and by the blessing of God, I was able to relieve the child. After supper, the governor showed me to a room in which was a real bed. This he told me I could use. As I had only twenty-four miles to travel the next day, I took advantage of this bed to the fullest extent, and was much refreshed.

We reached Guaicho, the border town of Bolivia, at four o'clock that afternoon. Over the line was Peru. We found a place to stay with the Indians, and I sent my guide to buy feed for the mules. He came back saying that no one in the village would sell him anything. We had to have feed for our mules, so I went to the village, but found the people very ill-tempered. They would sell me no feed.

I was wondering what to do, when a man came across the street toward me who seemed friendly. I addressed him; and as he answered me pleasantly, I explained to him my trouble. "Oh," he said, "you must go to the prefecto. This being a border town, every one is regarded with suspicion." We both went to the prefecto, and my new-found friend told him what I needed. The prefecto gave me an order for feed, and invited me to return and have supper with him. I did not promise, however, as I was very tired.

I secured the feed for our mules, returned to our Indian hut, took a refreshing bath in the river near, and determined to retire early. Just as we were about to sit down to our frugal repast, a messenger appeared, summoning me to the prefecto's house. I went, and found the prefecto and my new friend and two other head men of the village awaiting supper for me. They were all so very kind and sociable that I soon forgot my weariness; and as they seemed inclined to listen, I told them of our work, and what we intended to do for the Indians. The prefecto said: "Oh, that you would come among us! We need just such a work here." After a very pleasant evening, I departed, promising that I would remember them in our work for the Indians.

About four o'clock the next morning, I was awakened by an Indian boy calling to us through the door. I asked Stephen what the boy was saying. He said the boy was telling us that some one was stealing our mules. We jumped up quickly, and I threw a raincoat about me, as I had made myself comfortable for the night by removing my outer clothing. When I reached the road, I found Stephen struggling with two men, trying to regain possession of our mules. I grappled with them, telling them, at the same time, that I intended taking them to the prefecto's office. This seemed to make them more anxious than ever to get away, and finally one of them did escape.

As I was making ready to take the remaining man to the office of the prefecto, an army officer with six soldiers entered the yard, and in a very stern voice announced that I was under arrest.

"What for?" I asked.

"Because you have struck Bolivian soldiers," he said.

I explained to him about the attempt of the men to take our mules, and that I wanted to take the men to the prefecto.

"Well, you struck these men, and they are soldiers," he said.

I replied that I had not struck them, and called his attention to the fact that they were not hurt in any way, which would be hardly probable had I struck them. However, he insisted that I go with him.

As we were about to start, a well dressed man came running into the yard, and spoke in a low tone to the officer. Then they both came to me, and begged my pardon for what had occurred, scolding the two men for trying to take our mules, and asking them why they did so. One answered that he saw that the mules were "such good ones."

They then left me, and I thanked God for delivering me from what might have proved to be a long delay with much hardship. I could then see that He had guided in my

Meeting with the Indians—Always the Best of Attention

(195)

spending the evening with the prefecto, for it was he who had countermanded the order for my arrest. I afterward learned that in this country, it was the custom for soldiers, when they were on the march and needed saddle animals, to take them wherever they could find them, without asking permission; but it was usually from some of the Indians. The remainder of our time at this place was spent in tranquillity.

At three o'clock the next morning, we were up and on our way again; and at four-thirty in the afternoon, having traveled thirty-six miles over the rough road, we began looking for a place to stay overnight. We had not gone far, when I noticed a small Indian village away up on the mountain among the rocks. I asked our Indian brother to go and see if the people would receive us, and if they would, to wave his hat, and I would come on. I was glad to see him wave his hat.

I found the Indians very kind; and as they brought Stephen some food, they asked him if I would be offended if they brought me some. I understood, and told them that I would be very thankful for it. Indeed, I was hungry and cold, and the steaming food looked good to me. They were much pleased that I ate so heartily.

After supper, we held a meeting with the Indians, and they listened intently. Some threw away their coca-leaf mixture, the curse of the Indians. When I told them that Jesus was soon coming to reclaim His own, they could not restrain themselves any longer, but burst out with loud exclamations of *"Waliki! Waliki!"* meaning, "Good! Good!"

After the service, the chief came to me and asked when I would return to them. As we had so few workers, I answered that I could not tell.

"But I want to know when you will come to us again, and teach us all."

Again I told him that really I did not know, as this village was so far from our mission, and we were so few.

"Oh, but we must know," he continued.

Finally I said, "If I do not return, some one else will."

"But how am I to know that some one else will teach us the same things?"

I thought a moment, then picked up a small pebble, and broke it in two. I gave him one half, and told him that whoever should come to teach him and his people as I had taught them, would have the other half and bring it to him. He took his half and put it away very carefully, saying, "It is well." The sequel of this story will be told in another chapter.

They would take no money from us for their hospitality, but we gave them some very hard bread that we had. This they accepted with thankfulness. Many of them had never seen bread before.

The next day, we continued our journey. At midday, we had to cross a large river, and the Indians brought a small boat to take us over. These boats are made of grass; and when one of the mules got into one, there was not much to be seen of the boat. Yet they got us over to the other side safely.

When I proposed to settle with the Indians for taking us across, they demanded fifteen dollars. I knew that was an outrageous price. The usual charge for taking two persons across with two saddle animals would be about sixty cents. I tried to explain to the Indians that the price they asked was exorbitant; but the more I tried to explain, the angrier they became. They tried to seize our mules' bridles, and would not permit us to go on.

Indians Making Grass Boats

My guide told them, in the most eloquent manner, what our work was, and that we were friendly to the Indians, and what the missionary had been doing for those on the Puno side, and that our journey was in the interest of the Indians throughout the country. After this, they immediately calmed down, and said they would be satisfied with whatever we would give them.

We kept on until dark, but found no place to spend the night. We saw a storm coming on, and were getting anxious; but finally we came to an Indian hut, and asked for a place to stay overnight. The occupants told us they had no place except a very small hut with the roof partly torn off. We got into this just as the storm broke; but we could not rest, for the rain came through the roof, and the cold wind blew through the walls. By the flashes of lightning, we could see our saddle animals trembling with the cold; and as we were in the same condition, we thought it better to go on in the storm and darkness.

Our mules seemed glad to go. We picked our way along with the aid of a lantern; but the wind blew it out every little while, notwithstanding my endeavor to shield it, and I had difficulty in relighting it with my benumbed fingers. One time, when I was lighting the lantern, I remarked to my guide that it was too bad the light persisted in going out. "Well," he said, with a solemnly paternal air, "you must be careful not to let it go out." His manner struck me as so funny that I laughed in spite of the cold. We lost the road at times on account of the water. Still we kept on, and it was very interesting to me to see the way my Indian guide would find the road again. We had to pass along narrow ledges where a slip would mean positive death; but the angel of the Lord was with us, and we got through safely.

The next morning, we reached the great Quichua country. We stopped at the hut of a Quichua Indian, who treated us very kindly, giving us food, and also feed for our mules. The Quichuas seemed to be far more amiable than the Aymaras, and we were anxious to open a work for them also.

The following evening, we arrived at Puno, the end of our journey, having made the circuit around Lake Titicaca in three weeks.

CHAPTER XII

Proof of Appreciation

MESSENGERS now began coming in from the more distant provinces, pleading with us to open up mission stations in their localities, and furnish schools and teachers for them. As I was making ready to answer some of the most urgent of these calls, I was taken down with inflammatory rheumatism; and for three weeks, I suffered excruciatingly of this terrible disease.

Mrs. Stahl called in two Indian brethren to help take care of me during this sickness. As the Indians came into my room and saw me lying there, many would burst out crying. At one time, she said to some of the Indians who had called, "Do not forget to pray for my husband, that he shall be restored to health again." One of them replied: "We do pray for him. We not only pray for him during the day, but we go out on the plain every night at midnight and pray for him."

One Sabbath, a call was made for some of the Indians to bring milk to our house, Mrs. Stahl telling them that I was not able to eat any other food. The next day, they came.

After the Sabbath Services at Plateria

Across the plain and down the mountain side came hundreds of Indians, all with little jugs in their hands, which proved to be full of milk. Mrs. Stahl filled every available dish in the house, including the washtubs, and we had milk enough to bathe in.

One day, as I was lying there, five very tall Indians came in through the open door. They came to my bedside, and knelt there, and with pleading voices said: "Father, come over and help us. We also want to know the way."

I promised them that when I could get up from my sick bed, I would visit them.

"Oh," they pleaded, "have you no one to send now to teach us? We have brought our mules and pack animals with us, so that we can take the teacher right along."

I explained to them that we had no teachers, all those available having been placed in different provinces. Then they began to plead again, telling me how hard it was for them to return to their people without a teacher.

After a few moments, they turned to my son, twelve years old, and began to talk to him, asking him many questions.

Finally one of these big Indians came to me again, and said, "Let your little boy come over and teach us."

"Oh," I replied, "he is only a child yet, and is not prepared to teach."

"But," the man persisted, "if we only knew what he knows, we should be happy."

Then my son came over to me, and said: "Papa, let me go with them. I will be all right. I would enjoy teaching these people."

At another time, three messengers came from one of these high mountain regions, pleading for teachers; but we were not able to grant them. One of these Indians took out from under his shawl a large piece of silver, which he handed to me. "Now," he said, "if you will come and teach us, we will show you where there is much of this silver buried." Apparently the poor man supposed that I did not want to come, and he thought to tempt me by the offer of the silver.

When Mr. and Mrs. Rojas had been with us about a year, doing excellent work for the Indians, they had to leave very suddenly one morning for the coast on account of the effect the high altitude had on them. The school had just been opened, and they had it well in hand; and when the children found that their teachers had gone, many of them were in tears. But Mrs. Stahl volunteered to take the school, and the children were happy again.

Our work now became very heavy. The Sabbath attendance had grown to nearly eight hundred; and besides, the Indians were bringing their sick from greater distances. Finally I was compelled to answer importunate calls that came from distant places, where we expected to open mission stations as soon as more help should arrive. Thus Mrs. Stahl would be left alone with Luciano, our faithful Indian boy, to manage the home station, caring for the sick, conducting the two Sabbath meetings, and carrying on the large day school.

The governor of the mountain district of Pichacani had twice sent messengers urging me to visit him, and I felt that I could no longer refuse. So one morning early, accompanied by Chief Camacho and Juan Huanca, I started to the place. Our way led us through a very rocky section, to an elevation of fifteen thousand feet. Little grows up there, except a tough mountain grass. Yet the scenery is majestically beautiful. There

CHIEF CAMACHO AND JUAN HUANCA

(207)

is something fascinating about those great rocky cañons.

As we neared Pichacani, we received word that the town was in the midst of a drunken feast; and as we did not want to give the priests that were conducting the feast a chance to set the drunken mob on us, we decided to rest awhile out on the mountain, and arrive at the village at dark. Accordingly, we staked out our horses, and visited the ruins of an ancient mining mill near. As I went through those ruins, I thought, If they could only speak, what an awful tale they could tell!

There were great stone grinders still in place. These grinders were over five feet across and two feet thick. Thousands of Indians gave up their lives working in these mines, getting out gold for the Spaniards. As I viewed those ruins, I imagined I could see hundreds of half-naked Indians bringing the quartz from the mountain a mile away, hear the curses of the Spaniards, see the cruel lash fall, and every now and then a poor, exhausted Indian fall beneath his heavy load.

It is difficult to get an Indian to reveal where any of these mines are situated. They have taken every precaution to hide all trace

INCA RUINS, SOUTH AMERICA

of them, filling up the veins and the openings so that they would be hidden from view.

As the sun was sinking in the west, we prepared to continue our journey; but just as we were about to mount, Camacho's horse broke away and joined a group of half-wild horses on the plain. We spent some time recovering him. Then I discovered that in the chase, I had lost my field glass, so we all turned out to find it. This was not a light undertaking, as the plain was covered with grass five or six inches high. Soon a hailstorm put a stop to our search, and we decided to spend the night in an old hut near-by.

Camacho very much bewailed the loss of the glass, saying it was all his fault, because he had not taken better care of his horse. I told him, however, that he should not feel bad, as doubtless God had a purpose in this delay, and we should find the glass all right in the morning. We all felt that it would be better to reach the town in the morning, when all would be quieted down, as there are usually many drunken people on the streets of the towns on feast days.

The next morning, we arose early, and prepared to look for the glass and continue our journey. First we had prayer that God would help us to find the glass and prosper us on our way; for we know that God grants our requests in small matters as well as in great. We started out, and not more than ten minutes had passed when Camacho called that he had found the glass.

Then we set out for the village. As we entered, we met the governor, who had heard we were coming, and was on the lookout for us. He took us at once into his house. We found him a very sociable man, and much interested in our work. He wanted us to take charge of his village school, and also work in behalf of the Indians in his province. He said he had taken note of the Indians connected with the mission, and they seemed so clean and obliging, he wished that all the people of his province might be the same.

"They would be worth so much more to the country, and be more useful in every way," he said. "Now when I want to send an important message, I can hardly find a man that is trustworthy; and I wish I might have some of your Indians here to help me at times."

He asked about our religious belief, and was particularly interested in hearing of the soon coming of our Lord, who has gone before to prepare a kingdom for His children, and will put an end to all sin and suffering. As he listened, his face grew grave, and he said: "Would that all might know and believe this! Anything I can do to help you bring this message to my people, I shall be glad to do. Go out among the Indians here anywhere you like and hold your meetings."

After a lunch that he had provided for us, the mayor of the town and several other prominent men called. They took us through some of the ancient mines, and then through the old Spanish church. This church was erected shortly after the Spanish conquest. It was adorned most elaborately. On the walls hung large paintings representing different phases of the life of Christ. They were really beautiful; and for a few moments, I forgot myself, and started to explain to the people who had gathered in the church what each picture represented. Although they had seen these paintings many times, the questions they asked showed that they did not know what they represented.

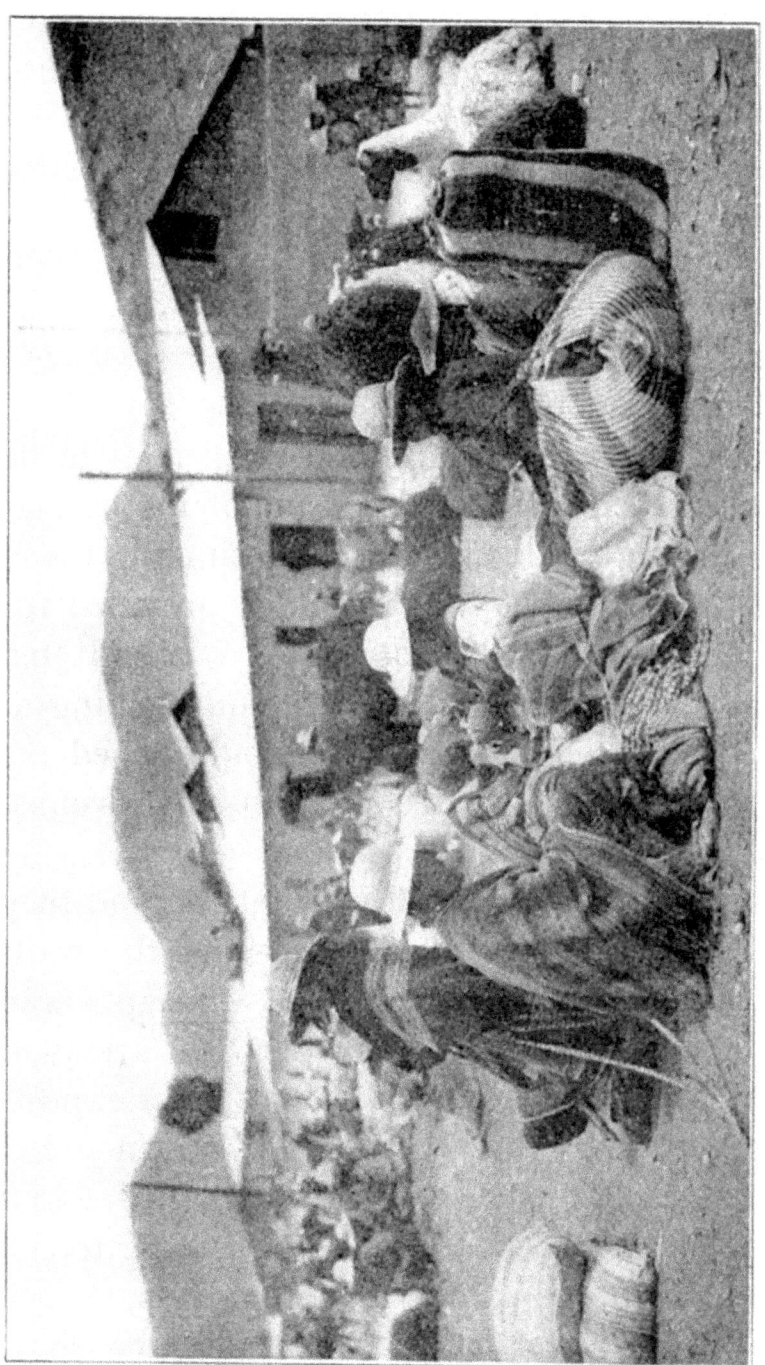

Lunch Time

After this, we took leave of the governor, the mayor, and others who were with us, and continued our journey. Everywhere, we found the Indians interested; and we held many meetings with them. In one of their large settlements, they came out to meet us with flags and drums, and escorted us to a hut they had prepared for our use.

One of the first things they asked us to do was to teach them to sing some of the hymns. After holding a meeting and singing many hymns, we partook of the lunch provided for us, and retired for the night. We had just fallen asleep when I heard a loud rapping at the door. I lighted a candle and opened the door, and in filed fifteen Indians, five women and ten men. The women were carrying heavy bundles, wrapped in blankets; and they seated themselves solemnly around the walls of the hut. One of the men, who appeared to be the chief, said: "Brother, we are glad you have came to us. We have been expecting you. We know that your journey has been long and hard, and that you are tired and hungry; so we have brought you some food." They then unwrapped the bundles, which proved to be earthen kettles containing food.

They had wrapped them in heavy blankets so that they would retain the heat, as they had come a long distance.

Although we had eaten heartily about an hour before, yet in order not to disappoint these Indians, we thanked them cordially, and told them we should be glad to partake of the food they had brought. They were very pleased indeed. As one of the women served the food into the bowls that we had, I would take a taste with my teaspoon, and hand the rest to my Indian guides, who were usually ready for an extra meal or two. In this way, I disposed of most of the food.

When these Indians left, we retired again for the night. We had but well gone to sleep when again there came a loud rapping on the door. Wondering what this could mean, I quickly arose and lighted the candle; and in filed some twenty other Indians, who had come from another district, farther away. Some of these also were carrying large bundles done up in blankets. When they had seated themselves, the spokesman said, "Brother, we know that you have come a long distance to visit us, and that you are tired and hungry, so we have brought you some food."

Not wanting to hurt their feelings by refusing their gift, I told them we were glad for the kind interest they had shown in our welfare; and as the women dished out the food, again I took a little with my teaspoon, and passed the remainder to my guides. But they refused it, saying they could eat no more; and for a moment, I did not know what to do. Finally I said to the Indians, that we should be glad to have them eat with us, as they too had come a long distance. We would taste of the food, then hand it around; and in this way we got rid of most of it. They seemed delighted, and said they were going to stay a day or two with us in order to attend the meetings.

After a few more days, we visited one of the highest Indian communities in that section. It is in a dreary place indeed, the wind sweeping over the mountain tops in a terrific gale most of the time. Nearly every afternoon, fierce hailstorms, accompanied by flashes of lightning, break over this mountain region. The Indians here are all tall, strong men, their faces hard-looking and seamed.

As we reached this district, the chief, a very hard-faced man, came out to meet us. He offered us one of his huts to stay in. "We knew that the missionary was coming to visit us," he said. It is remarkable how news is carried among these people. In the farthest mountain settlements, they are well informed as to what is taking place in the large towns where the market places are. When anything unusual occurs, the report is carried swiftly throughout the region.

This chief tried to make us comfortable in every way. In the morning, I asked him if our horses were safe. I had worried during the night about their safety, for we had heard that this wild mountain country was infested with horse thieves. He replied with a kind smile: "Yes, they are safe. I have been up all night watching them." He had himself taken the horses to a spot where he knew the grass was good, and watched them there while they fed.

The Indians of this section were greatly interested in the meetings. In one of these, this chief exclaimed: "Oh, how can we learn these things without a teacher! Send us a teacher, some one who can stay with us and teach us these things." When we prayed, he would prostrate himself on the ground in deep reverence.

As we were here caring for the sick and holding meetings with the people, I became very ill, having a high fever. I thought best to start for the home station at once, as we had a long distance to go over the mountains; and it was well that I did start promptly, for my illness proved to be typhoid fever. Four weeks I lay ill, my faithful wife caring for me. We were alone at the time.

Repeatedly I saw my wife weeping. I asked her why she wept; and finally she told me she had been reading a medical book, which stated that hardly any one forty years old would recover from typhoid fever. I had just turned forty a few weeks before. I said to her: "Never mind the medical book. The Lord holds life and death in His hand."

When I had been out of bed only three days, and was still very weak, messengers came from the village near, saying that there was sickness in the governor's family, and requesting me to come at once. I told them I was so weak I could hardly walk; but they implored me to come, and said they had brought a gentle, easy-riding horse for me.

PROOF OF APPRECIATION 219

Nothing would do but for me to go with them. When I reached the house, I nearly fell to the floor from sheer weakness. Still I ministered to those who were sick; and when I left them, the governor feelingly expressed his appreciation of our evident interest in his people.

CHAPTER XIII

The Broken Pebble

ABOUT this time, several large delegations of Indians came to us from the province of Moho. I have been wont to speak of this as the "broken stone" region, for here is where I divided a pebble with a chief at the time of my journey around Lake Titicaca, about three years before.

Moho is situated on the north shore of Lake Titicaca, and is made up of high, rocky mountains and fertile valleys. The journey from our main station, La Plateria, required four days on horseback and about ten hours by steamer. This province is composed of sixteen Indian districts.

As soon as I had recovered sufficient strength, I started out with guides and interpreters to visit this region. When the steamer on which we crossed the lake, arrived at the port of Moho, we found many Indians there to meet us. They took us to a house near. Soon others were seen coming from all directions. We held meetings at once, and the Indians were intensely interested. In the afternoon, a large delegation arrived from the

Family Group of Indians Near Lake Titicaca

district of Occa Pampa, twenty-one miles distant. They wanted to take us to their place straightway, but the Indians of the port would not consent to let us go until morning.

Early the next morning, we mounted the mules that had been brought for us, and started for Occa Pampa. We thought best to stop at the town of Moho on the way, and notify the authorities of our arrival, and tell them what our errand was, as large gatherings of Indians generally arouse their fears. By the time we reached the village, hundreds had gathered, cheering us as we went. I advised them to go on through the village and wait for us on the other side. Then I, with three others, visited the governor.

He received us in a very nervous manner, saying he had received word that we were coming. I told him that I had come to visit the Indians of the district, and that I wanted him to know my purpose. He listened very intently, and at the close, remarked that our work was not new to him. He said: "Don't you know that these Indians here are very, very bad people? You had better not open up work here. They are thieves, robbers,

Indian Officials, Called "Hilacatas"

drunkards, and very treacherous people to deal with."

"Good!" I responded.

He asked: "How is it you say 'Good'? Don't you know that these are the worst people in the world? They do not think anything of killing any one."

I explained to him that I had said "Good!" because, from what he said, I was convinced that we were in just the right place to open up gospel work. The very fact that these people were so bad was proof that they needed the saving power of Christ.

"Well," he said, "I wish you success then."

We found the people of the town not at all friendly. As we passed through, great crowds gathered, of both men and women, insulting us and threatening us. After leaving the town, and going on about six miles, we were stopped by a large company of friendly Indians, who were waiting on the road. These took us to a house near, where we held an enthusiastic meeting. We had to talk very loud, as a large crowd had gathered.

Among those present were some twenty chiefs — *hilacatas* they are called here. These men are the Indian authorities; and they are highly respected, even by the Spanish people. Each carries a rod of fine black wood, mounted with silver rings. They told us cordially that they had come to welcome us, and were glad that we had come.

One fine-appearing fellow stepped out, and said: "Sir, we are so far behind! We do not know the laws of the great God. We have been worshiping images, and we know they are not God. Come and teach us and our people. We are so far behind!"

We afterward held another meeting with them; and while we spoke, we saw many throwing away their cocaine mixture, and there were exclamations of approval throughout the gathering. Our meeting lasted two hours. Then the Indians of Occa Pampa insisted that we continue our journey to their place.

We mounted our mules, and proceeded on our way, accompanied by a large number of Indians on horseback and still more on foot. Clad in their many-colored blankets, they made an impressive sight as they filed through the cañons. About five o'clock in the afternoon, we met others coming to meet us, with flags and a band. When we reached our destination, an immense gathering was awaiting us. We dismounted amid cheers and great waving of flags, while the women showered us with the petals of small mountain flowers.

Nothing would do but to have a meeting at once. It lasted until dark. Never have I seen more enthusiasm than was shown in this district. Early the next morning, the people began bringing their sick. We treated one hundred and sixty patients that day. Most of them were afflicted with diseases caused by their unhygienic ways of living.

The following afternoon, a delegation of a hundred Indians came from a district called Wira Pata, begging us to visit them also. I had observed that each time we started out for a new district, we had different mules to ride. The mule brought for me this time appeared to be very nervous. I told the chief that I was quite content to use the one I had come in on, and asked if I might not retain him throughout my visit in this province.

"No," the chief said, "that would be impossible. We have arranged for you to visit eleven districts here. Each district has to

AS THE INDIANS OFTEN MEET OUR MISSIONARIES

(227)

help furnish the mounts and the food and bear the expense of this visit."

When I mounted this mule, he became more nervous still. He had no saddle, but merely a small blanket thrown across his back. I remarked to the owner that I believed this mule was going to throw me.

"Do not mind it if he does," the owner cheerfully replied. "As you are tall and the mule is small, just light on your feet. I have done so, many a time."

I assured the man that I would do the best I could to alight on my feet. As soon as we started out, the mule evidently changed his usual tactics. Instead of simply trying to throw me, he started to run away; and as he was galloping along, he suddenly turned a corner, and left me lying out on the plain. I was unhurt, however, and immediately got up; and the Indians furnished me a gentler beast.

The whole district, men, women, and children, came to meet us. The sight was an unusual one,— the men in their highly colored clothes, and the women in their deep black,— something that is not seen in any other district. Here again we were greeted with cheers and flowers.

The women of the district brought their children for me to bless. I told them that I did not have power to bless the children, but would ask Jesus to do so. They were deeply interested as I placed my hand on the children, and prayed God to bless them.

Here we had great difficulty in restraining the people from kneeling before us and kissing our hands, this being to them an act of worship. We forbade them, and pointed them to Him to whom alone worship should be rendered. They were indeed poor, needy people, given wholly to idolatry, filled with many strange superstitions. When we told them the simple gospel story, some of the women clapped their hands with delight.

We passed the night at this place, the Indians having made us very comfortable in a small hut, with skins and blankets. Long before daylight, a great crowd gathered before our door. We found that again the people had brought many sick for us to take care of; and as we treated their sick, we also told them how to prevent these diseases. They were very much interested in a faradic battery I had brought with me, which proved to be to them one of the wonders of the world, for they had never seen the like before.

The following day, we reached the large district of Paru; and at this place, we met the greatest number of people. While speaking, we had to have two interpreters, stationed in different parts of the crowd, as one could not be heard by all. We spoke two hours, after which we treated the sick that had been brought to us.

We spent several more days visiting the districts that the Indians had planned for us to visit. In all these places, we found the same enthusiasm for the gospel. When we came to the last district, the name of which is Umucho, I determined to visit the chief who had the other half of the "broken stone." I could not help thinking of the wonderful difference between the tour I was now making, and the one I had made three years before, alone with my guide. Little did I think, at that time, that I should be privileged to see thousands of the people in these places eager to hear the gospel. We have now in this district two large mission stations and seven day schools.

THE BROKEN PEBBLE 231

As we rode into the chief's yard, his wife ran out to meet us; and greeting me, she exclaimed, "Oh, why did you stay away so long?" I told her it was only about three years. But she said, "Yes, yes; it is at least twenty years since you were here before." I tried again to convince her that it was not more than three years; but she insistently replied, "Yes, it is more than twenty years ago," adding, reproachfully, "We have waited so long." I tried to console her; but somehow I wished that I had had opportunity to visit them before, especially when she told me, with tears streaming down her face, that her grown son had died since my first visit. So many things had happened in the short time I was away, no wonder the time seemed long.

The chief was not at home. His wife told me he had gone on a long journey, and that he would not return for some weeks. I asked her to let me see the half of the broken stone I had given to the chief. "Oh," she said, "I do not know where it is! The chief would not tell even me where he hid it."

When I told her that soon there would be a mission started near her, her face brightened up, and she exclaimed, "Oh, then we can come and hear; then we can get medicine for our sick ones."

She told me, in her sad way, that many, many years before, they had been a happy and free people; they had much better clothes to wear, much better food, in greater abundance, and the people did not use alcohol nor cocaine. I told her we were going to teach her people not to use alcohol nor cocaine, and were going to start schools for their children. She expressed herself as being very happy indeed, but said again, "Oh, we have waited so long!"

CHAPTER XIV

A Mysterious Rescue

A FEW weeks after returning from this trip, we were made happy by the coming of three capable young couples from America to help us in the work. These were C. V. Achenbach and wife, John M. Howell and wife, and R. Nelson and wife. While they were taking training at the home station, getting acquainted with the Indian work, my wife and I were left freer to go among the people in the more distant districts.

We decided to visit some of the districts where interests had been created. Three trusty Indians accompanied us. The first place we went to was the province of the Esquiñas. We had previously organized a school there, with an Indian in charge. We found them holding their school sessions out of doors, because enemies had demolished the school building one night a few weeks before.

Our next stop was Jollini, about fifty miles to the north of Esquiñas. When we had gone about thirty miles, we found some Indians waiting for us. They had heard that we were

(233)

coming to see them, and had been waiting in the road for a number of days. They accompanied us, running beside the horses, and easily keeping up with them the whole remaining twenty miles. It was after dark when we arrived. The Indians were delighted to see us, especially Mrs. Stahl, whom they had invited to visit them. They tried in every way to make her comfortable; but of course the best they have is very crude. We slept on the earth floor, and the mountain wind blew through the hut. Little grows in these high, cold regions, and we could not take much food in our baggage. It is a problem to get feed for the horses. But the Lord helps as we work for Him, even in the most trying conditions.

We held meetings every day with these people. We found them quite well informed in regard to the gospel, as our native worker, Luciano, had done excellent work among them for several months. Here we baptized twenty-five very dear people, and opened a school with seventeen pupils. We placed in charge a strong native worker, who had taken about two years' training at the home station. We left them very happy. "Now we have a

MR. AND MRS. STAHL ABOUT TO START FOR A VISIT AMONG THE INDIANS

(235)

real school and a real church," they said. They told us they were tired of idols, images of stone and wood and mud. One woman informed us that she had thrown the image of St. Peter into the lake two months before, and it hadn't returned yet, so she knew that it was no god.

One thing that makes an Indian happy above all other things is to learn that he, a poor, downtrodden Indian, can go to God just as he is, without first having to talk to dead saints about his needs.

Just before we left this place, an Indian came from Queñuani to guide us to his district. It is well that he did; for our road led through a twelve-mile swamp, and we could not possibly have picked our way alone over the soft ground.

We were much impressed with the advantages at Queñuani for reaching thousands of Indians. It had boat connection with Bolivia and with Puno, our railway station to the coast; and there was a large market located at Yunguyo, only three miles away, where the Indians of Bolivia came in great numbers to do trading. The Indians pleaded most earnestly that a missionary be sent to them, and

A MYSTERIOUS RESCUE

they wanted a school also. We promised to send them help as soon as we had any one to send.

While we were lecturing among them, and treating the many sick they brought to us, we heard rumors from the town near, that the priests were inciting the people to kill us. The Indians about us seemed to be quite nervous over the matter, and told us there was great danger that the priests would raise a mob against us; but we replied that as we now had religious freedom in Peru, there was no likelihood that harm would come to us, much less that we should be killed. We did not realize the viciousness and ignorance of the priests, nor to what extremes they would go.

After we had been there for nearly a week, one morning we saw coming toward us, away out in the valley, a great crowd of people. As they came nearer, we distinguished two priests leading them. Many of the people were on horseback, and some were armed with rifles and shotguns. As they came nearer, we recognized among the crowd men of authority from the towns about. We could not believe that harm was meant for us. Near us was a building where the priests usually held their religious feasts, and we thought they were coming to celebrate some such service.

We noticed Indians coming from all directions, until there were fully five hundred gathered together. The priests talked to them for two hours, and gave them alcohol to drink, then led them within one block of the hut where we were staying. Here they addressed the mob again, and we afterward learned that they were inciting the people to kill us, telling them it would be an honor, and that they would not be punished.

After talking to them about an hour, the priests set off what is called the *fugata,* a sort of large skyrocket, which is a signal, in these savage sections, for attack at a bullfight, or anything of that sort. What was our surprise to see that insane mob led by the lieutenant governor, the authority that should have protected us! He was mounted on a large horse, and was calling to the people to surround our house.

We thought even then that they were only trying to frighten us; but on they came, gathering large stones as they approached. Many were armed with long, steel-tipped whips and with clubs. The first thing they did was to cut loose our five horses, and stab them with knives, so that they ran frightened down a ten-foot bank, and galloped wildly off across the valley. I tried to stop the horses, but was attacked by some of the mob, and struck several times with stones. One stone wounded me severely on the head, and the blood blinded me. I almost fell; but Mrs. Stahl pulled me into the hut and closed the door, just in time to avoid another terrible volley of missiles.

In another moment, however, hundreds of stones crashed through the door, smashing it into bits; and the yard was filled with shouting, frantic Indians. We quickly piled our baggage in front of the opening in the door, to prevent them from forcing their way in. They were shouting now loudly in the Indian language, *"Pichim Catum,"* which means, "Catch them and burn them," all the while trying to push the baggage aside, and striking at us with their steel-tipped whips. The very fact that so many were trying to force their way in at one time, retarded them. Above the yelling of the Indians, we could hear the laughter of the priests.

In all this time, we had not forgotten to seek the Lord, and we were ready to meet death for Him if He so willed. I hastily wrote a few lines to our coworkers and children at the home station, asking them to go on with the work. Mrs. Stahl prayed with and comforted the two Indian women who were with us in the hut. Our three native young men were brave and true, and were only concerned for us. With great difficulty did I restrain Luciano from rushing out upon the mob. Had he done so, he would have been torn to pieces in a moment.

At this juncture, the priests called loudly to the Indians to set fire to the straw roof; and soon some were coming with torches to obey the command. One of them climbed up on a pile of stones to light the roof; but as he applied the torch, the Indian woman who owned the hut jumped up on the stones beside him, knocking him off, and pulled out the burning straw with her hands. Just as she succeeded in tearing out the last of it, she fell down, and some of the straw fell upon her bare head, burning her severely. She afterward proved to be a very important witness because of this.

At this moment, when others of the Indians were making ready their torches to set fire to

A MYSTERIOUS RESCUE 241

the hut, and we had given up all hope of rescue, the whole mob, priests and all, withdrew. We came out of the hut in time to see the priests mounting their horses quickly, and fleeing across the valley, the mob following them.

We asked a frightened-looking Indian who stood near why these people had fled so precipitately. He said, "Don't you see that great company of Indians coming, all armed, to defend you?"

I did not see them. I turned to Mrs. Stahl, and asked her if she did. She said, "No." The Indian insisted that there was a great army of Indians coming to help us. We looked around, but could see no one. We know now that God sent His angels in that form to rescue us. There is no other way to account for what occurred.

As I was feeling very weak from the loss of blood, I lay down on the floor of the hut to regain my strength. Just at dusk, an Indian woman came bringing our horses. She had followed them for six miles, running "in the strength that the Lord gave," as she herself expressed it. We quickly saddled our horses, mounted, and under cover of a fierce storm, left the place.

We suffered intensely from cold, and our clothing was wet through. But we rode on and on, the lightning sometimes blinding us, and at other times showing us the way. We had heard that the people in the next town also had risen up against us, having been influenced by the priests; so our Indian brethren led us by a road that did not pass near this place.

After we had gone about fourteen miles, Mrs. Stahl told me she was cold and weak, and feared she should fall from her horse, and not be able to go on. We had eaten scarcely anything that day. So we stopped out on the side of the mountain, spread our wet blankets on the snow, and thus passed most of the night. At daylight, we gathered up our frozen blankets, and continued our journey to the next large town, which was Juli, where we arrived about midday.

The authorities there had already been informed of the attack upon us, and were considerably exercised over the affair; and they promised to bring the guilty parties to justice. We did not push the matter, however,

HIGH MOUNTAIN INDIANS

(243)

because we believed that all was permitted for the advancement of the work, and we were of good courage. One of the largest mission stations we have is now flourishing near the place where we were attacked.

As showing how this occurrence was regarded by many Catholics even, I append a translation of an article published in the Puno *El Siglo* of June 21, 1916:

"CONCERNING THE CRIMES IN ONE OF THE VILLAGES OF THE PROVINCE OF CHUCUITO

"The scandalous events that have just happened in one of the villages of the Yunguyo district, profoundly exasperate the mind of every sensible person.

"The priests, Don Julio Tomás Bravo and Don Fermín Manrique, on the fifth of the present month, go to Queñuani, together with twelve citizens, heading a great multitude of Indians; they celebrate mass in the chapel; they preach to the ignorant multitude the extermination of the unfaithful; they frighten them into setting out to victimize Mr. Fernando Stahl and his wife, who are engaged in establishing a school for the native children, in the house of Clemente Condori. The mob break into the house, they attempt to burn it, they throw stones, they howl, they break the head of the Protestant missionary, who miraculously escapes with his life; with knives they hack and cut their horses, making flight impossible. Meanwhile, the Catholic priests, those sainted (?) men, with the instinct of Nero, rejoice over their work, laugh, and celebrate the mortifying and criminal scene.

"Such is the savage act which, to the shame of the province of Chucuito and of the republic, has been committed by those who style themselves representatives of that benignant apostle and martyr of humanity called Jesus Christ.

"Without any doubt, there will be none, however strong an apostolic and Roman Catholic he may be, who will fail to denounce and condemn the brutal outrages that have been committed, after the celebration of a mass in which justices of the peace, lieutenant governors, and other notables, implored the Most High to kill, rob, and burn the human *devils,* and this in the twentieth century and in the full light of day.

"Now we wish to know: What sentiments, what ideals, what passions, what motives, or what commands have been fulfilled or interpreted in this form?

"The Indian does not even forebode that his religious sentiments—if such name may be given the gross fanaticism in which the clergy have maintained him for so many centuries—may either suffer detriment or find support, in the inoffensive establishment of two Yankees, who generously cure sickness, dispense remedies, and teach the people to read, gratis; and who prohibit the vicious dances at the festivals, the use of alcohol and coca, etc.

"Is it perchance true that the doctrines of Christ authorize, teach, and give rules to burn, spoil, and kill those who do not believe in the holy Gospels?

"No! In its blessed teaching, we have the greatest liberty as concerns the observance and preaching of its doctrines. The Nazarene said, 'Let him that will, take his cross and follow Me.' So that whoever oppose these principles are nothing less than the eternal Pharisees, who also merit the *eternal punishment.*

A MYSTERIOUS RESCUE

"The passions of the people have not been aroused, however much they may be susceptible to exasperation, on being wounded in their pride, in their desires, or in the faith they profess. Their temperament and psychology are only too well known. They are not capable of assuming intemperate or criminal attitudes, in defense of or against questions whose consequences the majority do not understand, and of which the rest care little, and some have even clear ideas, about the benefits experienced by those of the evangelical mission, with the humanitarian work being done at La Plateria, for example.

"The motives which the assailants have had are not mysterious. This is clear: They have pretended to frighten the missionaries, by means of an infamous rabble, without understanding the high purposes of their adversaries. Or perhaps they have maliciously and ridiculously belittled their work, without taking into account their great moral strength, their powerful perception, and how unconquerable they are in their enterprises. But have these who projected the scandal, measured the results they could produce by inciting a wild, ignorant, and drunken mob to fall upon defenseless beings — or have they always taken into account that they feared the power of the devils? — It is a miracle that tragic consequences are not to be lamented at this time.

"In the disgraceful evil, no other force, then, has dominated than that which the worthless animal resorts to in his own stupid defense. It matters not whether it comes from the common priest or the highest church functionary.

"For more than three hundred years, the priests have kept the native race in the most deplorable and inhuman condition, reaping the profits of their work, worse than parasites. Nor can they or any one else say that the government is responsible for such a situation. The governing of the state has always been managed Jesuitically by them, who have never concerned themselves with establishing even a school to instruct the flock, which is their duty. The result is that they are to blame for the present situation: they have sold the sheep, and as Judas, they should pay for their sin and faults. It is only now that they are profoundly troubled by the awaken-

THE ISLAND OF THE SUN, LAKE TITICACA

ing of the race which for their own benefit they always wish to keep in subjection.

"If, as vicars of Jesus Christ and ministers of the holy mother church, they were moral, honorable, charitable, or even good spirits, they would merit respect, and would receive social consideration. But just look! They commit crime, robbery, and murder, to oppose the propaganda which they consider noxious, rather than rely on good example, doctrine, and virtue. It is clear that they must be denounced and repudiated.

"The same individual who at La Plateria joined in the attack with the imbeciles who accompanied Bishop Ampuero, to-day is committing assaults at the head of the armed band in Queñuani. Behold the fruit of impunity.

"The same one who in this city at least aided in plundering the church of St. Peter of its wrought silver, to-day directs the assault against the messengers of civilization. Behold the result of silence, of inaction, which sooner or later become accomplices of crime.

"The healing streams of the century have brought us the evangelists, those truly Christian spirits, who, better than the priests, have a respect for the images of the saints and the faith of their enemies, for they are charitable, or, more than that, philanthropic and humane. Let us help them in their blessed mission.

"Now we know that the priests, for the greater part, by their frequent scandals, criminally intermeddling with the interests and business of civil and political life, have made themselves intolerable. Let us curb them in their abuses, demanding penal sanction, with the respect due to men, the laws, order, culture, and foreign sentiments.

"If a clergyman commit crimes like the pickpocket, like the robber or assassin, let him learn morality behind the bars of the prison, since from the pulpit he preaches iniquity.

"And if the evangelists show themselves irreverent, disrespectful, or if they demoralize and corrupt the Indians, denounce them without leniency before the constituted authorities. The laws guard, constrain, and protect everybody equally.

"June 18, 1916.

"(Signed by)

"Some Catholics that have always repudiated the attitude of the priests."

We cannot expect to go on with a work of this kind without meeting serious opposition from Satan, as he is angry when he sees the truth taking hold of hundreds of these poor, deceived Indians, and corruption and wickedness giving way to pure lives. "Go," is the command; and on we shall go in the strength of the Lord.

Those two priests have since died. Priest Manrique called upon us for help in his last illness. Everything possible was done for him, but it was of no avail. Priest Bravo, as yet a young man, and the leader of the assault at Queñuani, died at Moho in June, 1919, of a terrible fever, with only a few Indians to wait upon him; and because of fear of contagion, no friends accompanied his remains to the grave, three Indians having been hired for that purpose.

CHAPTER XV

Enemies Disarmed

WE were now able to establish four new mission stations, and we found that persecution was growing less and less. Some of our former enemies from the villages near were sending to us for medical help.

A messenger came from a village some distance from the home station, asking me to attend a sick family at that place. As I called at the house, a servant opened the door, and the host approached me, asking if I remembered him. I confessed that I had no recollection of having seen him before. "Well," he said, "I was subprefecto in Puno five years ago, when you and another man called upon me, and I did not treat you very kindly." I remembered him then, but he had greatly changed in looks.

Elder J. W. Westphal and I had called upon this man in the interest of our Indian work; and as we explained it to him, he became very angry, savagely shaking his fist in our faces, and told us he would do all he could to hinder us. I had lost sight of him since.

as he was removed from his post shortly after our visit.

He said further, "At that time, I got out petitions against you and your work." He told me of other things he had done to injure us, that I had not even suspected. Finally he said: "Now I know better. In fact, I wanted to tell you long ago that I was sorry, and have wanted to visit you; but each time, my courage has failed, and I have passed by your house."

He said he was now our friend, and had been such for some time. I assured him I was glad to meet him as a friend. I told him that naturally, at the time, I felt bad, but that God had turned all opposition for the good of the work. I have since been in his family many times, helping them in their sicknesses; and he has kept his word, and has proved to be a stanch friend.

Not long after this, I received a call from the village that had been foremost in persecuting us. The messenger came at midnight, rapping loudly on the door. I hastily got up and went to the door, and he imploringly said: "Please come at once. One of the prominent men of the village is very ill."

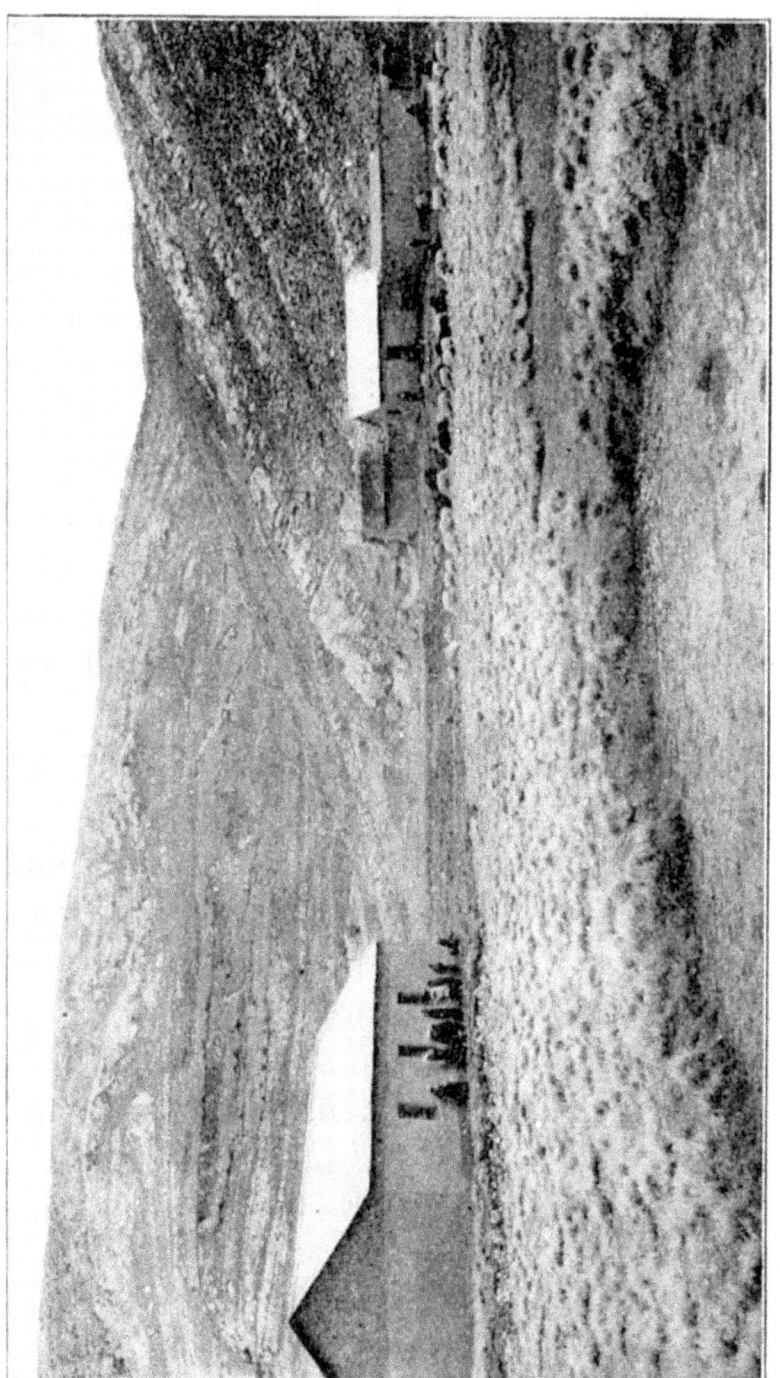

OUR SECOND MISSION STATION

I asked, "Who is it?"

"Oh, it is one of the prominent men there," he said, evading my question.

I dressed, and taking up the saddle bags in which I kept my medicines, started out of doors. He said: "You do not have to bother about saddling your horse. I have brought an extra horse for you."

I mounted, and the messenger led the way at a furious pace. We had twenty miles to go, but he did not spare the horses. Repeatedly I asked who the sick man was; but the messenger always cunningly evaded my questions.

As we rode into the village, we were met by three men, the mayor, the governor, and the judge of the district. I dismounted, and shaking hands, inquired who the sick man was. At my question, they appeared to be very nervous, and avoided answering directly, saying that the man had been sick for some time, and now had taken a dangerous turn, and asked if I would come and take care of him.

"Why," I answered, "that is what I came for."

"Well, we didn't know," they said, "whether you would take care of him or not."

"Most assuredly I will. That is what I came for," I repeated, "and every moment is valuable if this man is as ill as you say he is."

Finally the judge said, "It is the priest, Molino."

I confess that at the mention of that name, I was taken aback somewhat for an instant, because some weeks before, the priest named had incited a mob of Indians to kill us. But I answered almost immediately: "I am here to do all the good I can. Lead the way. I am very glad to take care of this man."

They then quickly led me into the priest's house, and into his room, where he lay suffering most intensely. I was able, by the blessing of God, to relieve him of his pain in a few moments. He thanked me over and over again, telling me of the terrible agony he had suffered for the past three days.

I informed the priest that he would need an operation to effect a permanent cure, and that the best thing he could do was to go down to one of the large coast cities, where he could get surgical help. He consented to do this; and as I was about to leave him, he said: "Oh, do not leave me, please! Stay with me, and go with me to the railway station." I assented.

He immediately gave orders for a bed to be made, upon which he could be carried to the railway station, two days' journey from this place. Then some forty Indians were called together to act as carriers. The following morning, we started out, the Indians, as they carried the priest, relieving one another without stopping. We were accompanied by ten of the most prominent men of the village.

The priest insisted that I ride his horse, and keep close beside him. Every once in a while, he put out his hand to see if I was still by his side. As we hastily made our way along the road, through the thickly populated districts, the people stared at us in open-mouthed astonishment; and in one village, I heard some exclaim in great surprise, as they recognized us both: "What is this we see? Is the priest the prisoner of the evangelist, or is the evangelist the prisoner of the priest?"

Late in the night of the second day, we reached the railway station. When the train pulled in, I helped the priest aboard, tucked the blankets around him, and gave him some medicine that would relieve his suffering until he should reach his destination. He went down to the coast city and had his operation, and in two months returned to his district a well man, and very friendly to us.

Other priests of that same district were not friendly, however, and did all they could to keep the people from us, but without success. When they called us devils, and told the people to have nothing to do with us, the people would only laugh at them, and say: "Oh, you want to keep us away from a good thing! When you get sick, you'll call the evangelist right away." And so the priests lost their influence throughout that district.

Besides the main station at La Plateria, we have now (1919) three other large mission stations in charge of missionaries from the United States, and two substations in charge of Indians, who have been trained at La Plateria. At each of these stations, there is a large school. In addition to these, we have in neighboring provinces twenty other schools for the Indians. There are over two thousand children in daily attendance in these schools. Over 1,500 Indians have been baptized, and thousands more are studying the gospel, preparatory to being baptized.

The great need is, men and means to forward the work. That is the only lack. We have the open doors. The teacher that comes here does not have to advertise. He no more than lands when a crowd takes possession of him and carries him off as their teacher. One of the prime needs is a training school wherein Indians can be trained to become efficient laborers for their own people.

The Indians who give up the use of alcohol and cocaine soon have means, which they use to buy better clothes, and to furnish their little huts with some very necessary articles, like tables, dishes, knives, forks, and spoons. On these little tables in the Indian huts now may be seen hymn books, Bibles, literature of the day, and schoolbooks for the children.

Communion Services Among the Indians

CHAPTER XVI

The Quichuas Calling for Help

FOR over a year, Quichua Indians had been coming to us from the immense district of Sandia and the province of Cuzco, asking for teachers to come and teach them as we had been doing for the Aymaras. There are over a million and a half of these Quichua Indians living in the Cuzco and Sandia regions. In their habits, they do not differ from the Aymaras; but they are of a milder disposition.

Up to 1917, our work had been altogether for the Aymaras. We were not able to meet all the calls from them; and that is one reason why we had delayed entering the Quichua territory. Even at the present writing (1919), there are among the Aymaras many districts that are waiting patiently for a teacher. Every day or two, some Indian comes and asks us, "Has our teacher come?" They are determined to get the next teachers as soon as they arrive on the ground. They are watching so closely that it would be impossible to smuggle a teacher over to the Quichuas, even if we wanted to do so.

When the Quichuas first came to this mission, they would stand at a distance; but when we smiled at them, they came into the mission yard, and we would welcome them, and in every way make them feel at home.

I had often wondered what we would do for an interpreter when we were ready to go among the Quichuas; but God provided. A few months before they began coming to us, an old Quichua came along one day with his son, and asked permission to place him in our day school. We were pleased to receive the

THE FIRST MESSENGERS FROM THE QUICHUAS

young man. He advanced rapidly, and has proved a jewel. He went with me on my first trip among the Quichuas, and did excellent work, showing a real interest.

When the first messengers from this tribe came to us, we were so busy that we were not able to visit them. But more and more messengers came, imploring us to go to their distant district. At one time, five came from Sandia, seven days' journey over the mountains, and arrived just as we had left the mission to take a trip among the Aymaras. When they were told that we would be gone for three weeks, they simply said, "We will wait until they come back, because we cannot go without them this time."

When I returned from my journey, and saw how anxious these people were to have me visit their district, it touched my heart; and, although I was tired, and much work was waiting for me, I prepared to go with them the very next day.

The fifth day we were out, we reached the town of Cojata, situated at an altitude of fourteen thousand feet above sea level. The ground was covered with snow, and the air was very cold. The sixth day, we crossed the great divide, at seventeen thousand feet. The weather was bitterly cold, and a blizzard was raging. Our faces were cut with the driving snow, and our lips were bleeding.

My mule, Samson, began to bleed from the mouth; and the other one bled at the nose. To make matters worse, the snow soon hid the trail. There are many warm springs on this mountain table-land; and as the snow hid them from sight, our animals would often plunge into one, and become fast in the mire. After several experiences of this kind, the mules became so nervous we had hard work to make them go forward. When we got into one of these miry places, the best thing to do was to force the animals through it, and get across to the other side, if possible.

Once we found, when we reached solid ground, that we were in a trap. All around us was a wide stretch of this miry ground. We could not return by the way we had come, because the water had risen and melted the snow, making it much worse than before. Our Quichua guides made the circle several times, trying to find a place where we could get out. Finally one of them said he thought he had found a way by which we would be

Among the Indians of the High Mountain Region, Elevation 16,000 Feet

able to reach solid ground. When we came where he was, we noticed little islands, as it were, about two feet across and five feet apart. The mules would be able to jump from one of these to another, and make the other side.

But I was deeply concerned about my mule Samson. He was a high-spirited animal, and of powerful build, and had a will all his own. I wondered whether I could make him jump from one of the islands to another. One of the guides got his animal over all right; and as I was worrying about starting mine, suddenly, without a word from me, Samson made one desperate leap, and landed on the first island, then jumped to another, then to the third, and then on to solid ground, before I had a chance to get a second breath.

I have had a better opinion of mules ever since. They certainly have good common sense. And I want to say, right here, a word about that mule of mine. He has taken me thousands of miles over these mountains, and has never failed me. Often, after observing his faithfulness, and his grit and courage, I have breathed a prayer, "Lord, make me as faithful in my sphere as Samson is in his."

If there are to be any animals in the kingdom of heaven, I hope that dear old Samson will be there.

That night, we slept in an old, dilapidated hut. I say we slept, but in fact we could not

"Treasures of Snow and Hail"

sleep. The wet snow kept coming through the roof, and after a few hours, it became so cold we could not endure it any longer, so we decided to continue our journey. The following day was a repetition of the day before. The snow continued to fall, and the trail was lost to sight. Only by the course of the mountain range could the guides tell the way.

In the afternoon, however, we reached the end of the high plateau over which we had been traveling, and started to go down. We had found the trail again. After a few hours' hard riding, we entered a small valley. The road led beside a mountain torrent, on each side of which were Indian huts. Soon Indians began to gather, gazing at us in fear and wonder, until our guide called to them in a loud voice. Then there was great excitement. The guide had told them that I was the missionary. They had been expecting me; and they began to run in every direction, calling to others. Some ran ahead of us. Our head guide himself became so excited that he started off on a gallop, leaving us to find our way the best we could.

A turn in the road revealed a large Indian house on the other side of the river, with many Indians gathered near, and some standing upon the roof. I concluded that this must be the place where we were to stop, and in this I was right. When I had dismounted from my mule, Indian men, women, and children threw their arms about me with loud exclama-

Indian Teachers Now in the Field

(269)

tions of joy. I had never received a warmer welcome in all my life. This reception made up for many of the hardships I had suffered on the way. As this was my first experience with the Quichua Indians at close range, it encouraged me to believe that our work would make progress among them.

The days that followed seemed to bear out this hope. The people enjoyed the singing, they took delight in the Word of God as it was explained to them, and in prayer they gave the most reverential attention.

They had erected a new hut especially for my use. The old chief took me by the arm and led me into this hut; and I saw that it had been plastered,—something the Indians do not usually do to their own houses,—and that there was clean straw on the floor. The chief said: "Father, we have built this house for you. We want you to stay with us a year." I replied that I couldn't stay with them so long. I told him of the sick people I had to care for, and of the other work I had to do.

"Well," he said, "then stay six months."
"Oh," I said, "I couldn't stay six months."
Then he got down to three months. I

THE QUICHUAS CALLING FOR HELP

finally told him that I would stay with them a few weeks, and would return to them as soon as possible, and perhaps bring a teacher to stay with them. This seemed to satisfy them.

The meetings that followed were wonderful occasions. The Spirit of God was present in a marked manner. Hearts were impressed, and many believed on the Lord Jesus. In one of the meetings, an old chief was standing in the middle of the crowd, and I noticed that tears were streaming down his cheeks. Suddenly he raised his hand, and exclaimed in a loud voice: "O my people, heaven has come to us! This is nothing less than heaven that has come to us!"

I had heard many strong expressions among these poor heathen people in my nine years of work for them, but never had I heard another expression that affected me quite as this one did. To be a messenger to bring heaven to the people is something to be glad for. These words have kept ringing in my ears ever since, and have been the means of spurring me on to more faithful work.

CHAPTER XVII

In Perils Oft

AS we were making preparation to return to Plateria, after a stay of a few weeks among the Quichuas, two messengers came running in one evening, and said excitedly that the priests from the town of Sandia, twenty-four miles distant, were inciting the people to come and kill us, and that the authorities were uniting with these priests, and were gathering soldiers to arrest us on the charge of inciting the Indians to rebellion against the government. The messengers told us that even at that moment, the mob was doubtless on the way.

After the experience we had in Queñuani with the priests, I had no more doubt of what they were able to do; so we quickly packed our goods, and started on our homeward journey, the Indians leading us out of the valley by a trail that did not pass near the villages. It was well they did this, as I afterward learned that only two hours after we had left, the great mob arrived, headed by eight soldiers who had orders to arrest us. It took them some time to find which way we had gone, as the Indians refused to tell them; and when they did find out, we were already out of their district. Then the Indians who had housed us, and many who had attended the meetings, were taken prisoners, driven to the village twenty-four miles distant, and put in jail. Some were placed in stocks, and some were beaten and received no food. Over fifty were thus treated, we were informed by messengers that escaped the guards and came to us two weeks afterward.

We avoided all the villages, and slept in the mountains. The third day, we encountered a very dangerous trail, not more than two feet wide in some places. We had to dismount, as there was not room for us to pass mounted. Our knees would rub against the wall of rock on one side, and we had to be extremely careful not to fall down the frightful precipice on the other side. We had thirty miles of this kind of trail. I walked ahead to look out for a place to pass in case we should meet any one coming from the opposite direction.

All went well until we were almost to the end of this narrow trail. Then we saw some mules coming toward us, loaded with rolls of sheet iron, evidently going to an interior mine. We found a place where, by pulling our animals' heads aside, and compelling them to place their fore feet up on the high bank on the side of the road, we could barely make room for the loaded mules to pass. There were seven of these mules. Three of them passed safely; but as the fourth came along, our black horse, Night, became frightened, and struggled to get away from the Indian that was trying to hold him. Suddenly his hind feet went over, and he plunged down the precipice, sometimes rolling a few feet, then bounding from one ledge to another like a ball, landing at times on his feet, and again on his back.

Far down the mountain side, he finally stopped. I clambered down as fast as I could, fully believing that almost every bone in his body had been broken; but as I came near him, he made an effort to rise. By a word, I warned him to lie still. If he did not, he would fall some five hundred feet farther before reaching the bottom of the cañon. I very carefully removed from him the remains of the saddle and ropes, and on examination, found that he did not seem to be injured in any way. It was a miracle.

The question now was, how to get him back up to the road. One of my Indian guides had come down to me by this time; and we finally decided that the only way was to zigzag along the steep mountain side. We were obliged to go long distances before we could find a place wide enough to allow us to turn around. In order to keep our balance, we had to go very fast. I went ahead, leading the horse; and I requested the boy not to spare the whip, but to keep the horse running.

In this way, after several hours of hard work, we finally reached the last part of our climb. Another hundred feet of running would bring us to a place four feet or more straight down from the narrow road. I told the guide that as soon as we should arrive at this steep place leading to the road, he should make an extra effort to compel our horse to make the last jump; for if he did not succeed in getting up on the road, he would again be dashed down into the gorge.

The Indian realized the situation. And it seemed that the horse also understood it; for when I, with one great effort, had jumped up to the road, and the guide called loudly to the animal, applying the whip unsparingly, the horse, with a wild scramble, secured a footing on the road.

Soon we entered the thickly populated district of Limbani. When we arrived at the town of Crucero, there was a drunken feast in progress. I had seen many of these religious feasts before, but never had I seen one carried on in quite the way this one was. To be out in the streets was dangerous to one's life. The fighting was horrible to see. Every few minutes some one would be carried from the crowd in a terribly wounded condition. I asked what feast it was, and was told that it was the feast of "Saint Rosa."

I felt like weeping as I saw these hundreds of poor, deceived Indians. They thought they were serving God in all this. I knew, from experience in the past, that there were many really noble people among them, and I longed to see the day when gospel teachers would be placed among them.

I thought of the many Indians at the home mission, who formerly had acted in the same way; and now hundreds of them were sane in mind and well in body, and were praising the living God for the saving gospel of Jesus Christ. I thought of Luciano — how, after he was baptized, and had been walking in newness of life for about two years, his people came to him, and demanded that he give up all, threatening that if he did not, he would be disinherited. I remember well how he came to me at that time, and asked what he could do to help his people. Finally he went to them one night, and called them together, and told them earnestly that he never would give up Jesus, but that he was willing to give up all for Jesus. In less than one year from that time, all his people had accepted Christ, because of Luciano's steadfastness.

At another time, when he was with me on a journey, we stopped in a village to take care of some sick people in the public plaza. The judge of the village came up to Luciano, and demanded roughly of him what he would have been if the missionary had not got hold of him. Luciano looked up at the judge, and solemnly replied: "Oh, what *would* I be! What *would* I be! What are all these poor Indians around here? I would be in a drunkard's grave to-day."

Luciano, Our First Indian Pastor, and His Wife
(278)

I thought of Antonio Alberto, a stalwart young man who consecrated his life to God, and who carried his books around with him to study, so that he could become a teacher for his people; and how, during vacation, he went down into the tropics of Peru, a seven days' journey from his home, and worked in those malarious swamps, in order to get money to carry on his studies. As he was returning with his father, who had gone down for him, he suddenly became very sick; and when they reached the high mountain regions, he could go no farther. Lying there beside the road, on those dreary mountain slopes, dying, he reached into his bosom, and took out a small bundle of money, which he handed to his father, and said, "Father, promise me that when you reach home, you will take the tithe of this money to the mission, for it belongs to God." This

Honorato, Rescued by the Gospel from Deplorable Darkness, and Now a Teacher Among His Own People

young man's last thoughts were of his duty to God. His father buried him by the roadside where he fell; and I am sure that in the day of resurrection, when the angels of God gather the elect from the four corners of the earth, Antonio's lonely grave on those mountains will not be forgotten.

I thought of old Brother Salas and his wife, who were leaders in the dances for many years. His head was marked with a hundred scars from the many battles he had taken part in; and when we first met him, he was almost insane from the use of cocaine. At the very first meeting we held among the Indians, he threw away his coca leaves; and both he and his wife exclaimed, "Oh, if we had only known this before!"

I well remember the struggle these old people had with the cocaine habit — how, when the fierce longing for the drug came upon them, they would come to us with the sweat streaming down their faces, and we would kneel with them, and pray the Lord to take from them the awful craving. Well do I remember when the victory came to them, and how, in the next prayer meeting, when we gave the Indians opportunity to testify, Salas arose, and reverently lifting up his face to heaven, said: "Oh, I thank Thee, Thou God of heaven and of earth, for the hope of the great beyond, and for deliverance from sin. I thank Thee for what my ears have heard about Thy Word. Blessed be Thy holy name. My days are few upon this earth, but I have in my heart the joy of meeting my Saviour soon." To see that face, so expressive of love, thankfulness, and holiness, was recompense for much that we have had to endure in taking the good news of salvation to this neglected race.

When we first opened the mission, people sneered at us, and said: "Oh, these Indians are worse than beasts! They will not be steadfast." But those who spoke thus, reckoned without God and His keeping power. Over fifteen hundred Indians have been baptized; and in all these years, I do not know of one who has deliberately given up the gospel. Again the scoffers said, "These Indians cannot comprehend the gospel." But the Lord says, "The entrance of Thy words giveth light; it giveth understanding unto the simple;" and that statement has been proved true with these people.

In connection with this, Maria, a beautiful Indian girl of eighteen, comes to my mind. This young woman had been a regular attendant at the prayer and Sabbath meetings for many months; but one Sabbath, she failed to appear. I made public inquiry about her; and one man said, "Why, Maria has black smallpox."

The next morning early, my wife and I mounted our horses, and with a guide, climbed up the steep mountain side. This took us several hours. Then we crossed a plain over twelve miles wide, and after that, went down a steep descent — so steep that we were obliged to place our saddle girths well back in order that our saddles should not slide over the horses' heads. After we had gone down several thousand feet, we crossed another wide plain, fording two rivers on the way; and finally, late in the afternoon, we came to a little hut there in the midst of the mountains. The guide said, "Here is where Maria lives."

When we entered the hut, and our eyes became accustomed to the darkness within, we saw Maria lying on the floor at one side of the room. We called her name, and she raised herself up, and made as if she would embrace

PERUVIAN WOMAN

us; then, thinking of her terrible disease, she fell back on her bed.

"Oh," she said, "I am so glad you have come to visit me! I am so happy in Jesus! I am going to die, but I am not afraid." Then she exclaimed, "Oh, sing some of those beautiful hymns to me, and pray with me now!" We prayed with her, and sang with her, and she joined in with her feeble voice. When we arose to go, she saw that we were weeping, and she said: "Do not weep, do not feel bad for me, because I am not afraid. I am going to sleep in Jesus; and on the resurrection day, I shall see you again." The last word that she said to us, as we went out of the little door, was, *"Ha-ki-sin-ca-ma,"* which means, "Until I see you again."

Who can say that this Indian girl had not grasped the great plan of salvation? Who can say that she did not comprehend the gospel? A few days after we were there, she died; but we know that when the Life-giver shall appear, He will raise Maria to immortal life.

How many times these things have inspired us to be more faithful, and to go on teaching the people! How many times they have kept up our courage when we were suffering cold and hardship in our work high in these mountain ranges! Can you wonder that our hearts bleed as we look upon the hundreds still in darkness? Who would forbid us to continue in this gospel work? Who can turn away their ears from the cry of the heathen in these dark lands, calling after Jesus, calling for teachers?

May the Spirit of the Lord impel many young men and young women to give up their worldly ambitions, consecrate their lives to God, and go out into these needy fields, among the people who have never heard the beautiful story of the cross. May the Lord impress many who cannot go out into these lands, to give liberally of the means intrusted to them, that this gospel work can go on. Oh, that teachers may be sent into these regions! Shall we stop now? Shall we leave these heathen without opportunity to know the living God? I am sure you will say, "Go on with the work for these children of Christ who sit in darkness."

CHAPTER XVIII

Supplementary Notes

GATHERED FROM VARIOUS SOURCES

THE beginning of the Lake Titicaca Mission was the conversion of the Aymara Indian Camacho. He was called to the army when young, and there of necessity learned the Spanish language. Reading created a hunger for more knowledge, which was fed by a skeptical, anti-Catholic Spaniard he met in the army. The Spaniard was compelled by his enemies to leave the country, and he went to London. He corresponded with Camacho through a friendly Catholic shoemaker named Peralta. Finally in London the Spaniard became converted to the true gospel message; and he sent publications thereon to Peralta and Camacho. After various trials, Camacho accepted the truth, and was baptized in 1910. Later Peralta also accepted the truth.

Camacho opened a school for the Indians about 1909. This was the beginning of mission work in the Lake Titicaca basin, and from this the mission has grown to a member-

LAKE TITICACA COLPORTEURS' INSTITUTE HELD IN 1919

ship of 1,500 or more, with thousands of others directly or indirectly affected by it for the better. Not long after the opening of Camacho's school, Mr. and Mrs. Stahl began their work among the Indians. It is well to remember that the Titicaca Mission, the field of Pastor Stahl's labors, does not include all the old Inca empire; it is but a part of that field, the whole being covered by the Inca Union Mission. There are millions of Indians outside the Titicaca basin who are reaching out for God.

Between the years 1915 and 1918, the following workers responded to the earnest appeals of Pastor Stahl and others for that field: Pastor and Mrs. C. V. Achenbach, Professor and Mrs. J. M. Howell, Mr. and Mrs. Reid S. Shepard, Mr. and Mrs. R. A. Nelson, Mrs. and Mrs. Ellis P. Howard, Mr. and Mrs. L. J. Barrowdale, Mr. and Mrs. Orley Ford, Mr. and Mrs. David Dalinger.

There are two native ministerial licentiates, Luciano Chambi and Juan Huanca, besides a score or so of native teachers. The last S. D. A. Year Book (1919) gives the following organization of the Lake Titicaca Indian Mission:

Territory: Departments of Puno, Madre de Dios, in Peru; and that part of the basin of Lake Titicaca which is in Bolivia.

Address: Casilla 28, Puno, Peru, South America.

OFFICERS

Mission: Superintendent, F. A. Stahl; Secretary and Treasurer, Reid S. Shepard; Executive Committee, F. A. Stahl, Reid S. Shepard, C. V. Achenbach, J. M. Howell, Ellis P. Howard.

Educational Department: Superintendent, J. M. Howell.

Home Missionary Department: Secretary, Reid S. Shepard.

Ministers: F. A. Stahl, C. V. Achenbach.

Licentiates: Reid S. Shepard, J. M. Howell, E. P. Howard, L. J. Barrowdale, Orley Ford.

Missionary Licentiates: David Dalinger, Mrs. F. A. Stahl, Mrs. C. V. Achenbach, Mrs. Reid S. Shepard, Mrs. J. M. Howell, Mrs. E. P. Howard, Mrs. L. P. Barrowdale, Mrs. Orley Ford, Mrs. David Dalinger, Luciano Chambi, Juan Huanca.

Mr. and Mrs. Nelson were compelled to leave the field because of the illness of Mrs. Nelson.

Pastor Stahl was away from the mission on a furlough during the year 1918. His visit to the United States aroused great interest in his field. In the last few weeks of his stay, he hastily prepared the manuscript for this book.

Mrs. Howard writes of the curiosity awakened by the little portable organ Pastor Stahl took back with him from the States. It has been of great help in getting access to the wild Indians.

The Umuchi Mission recently opened with Luciano Chambi in charge, now numbers over two hundred members. The last baptism reported was 49.

When Pastor Stahl was in this country, a boat was donated for work on Lake Titicaca. The Indians were told of it, and were told also that a boathouse would have to be built of stone. The next day, two hundred or more Indians came with ox teams and burros, and hauled rocks and carried stones sufficient for the building. A dinner for them followed, of which three hundred were partakers.

The Sabbath school at Plateria numbers about seven hundred; and there are but ten teachers, eight of whom are Indians. Some classes number over seventy-five.

Mrs. Stahl's nursing of the daughter-in-law of the president of Bolivia won the support of that gentleman in our work.

Fernando Osorio, teacher of our parochial school in Lima, Peru, in the *Review and Herald* of December 26, 1918, wrote thus of the influence of our work upon public men:

"The president of the Committee for the Improvement of Public Instruction, Dr. Vincente Villarán, through the recommendation of Mr. Encinas, of Puno, invited Elder E. F. Peterson, Brother H. B. Lundquist, and Brother F. C. Varney to explain the method employed in our schools of Plateria, which are called model schools by Señores Encinas and Villarán. The best elements of the university and of the Congress have a very live interest in our work for the Aymara Indians. They say that it is a marvel that the Indians learn habits of cleanliness and are becoming civilized so quickly under the influence of the Adventists, while for centuries under the Catholic Church they have done nothing. They already know the reason — the Holy Bible. . . .

"The Plateria Mission on the shores of Lake Titicaca has exercised a wonderful influence in all Peru. . . .

"There are other bills before the Peruvian Congress regarding civil marriages, and permitting Protestant churches to hold property; and Catholics are working against them."

Professor W. W. Prescott, of Washington, D. C., was in the Titicaca Mission, visiting it as field secretary of missions, when this religio-legal question was agitated. At that time, protest was made against Mr. Stahl's mission, and the awful *wrong* of which he was regarded as guilty was that he taught the Indians to settle their own difficulties among themselves instead of paying out so much money for lawyers and lawsuits. But that is just what all Christians ought to do — settle their own difficulties.

Among the riches first found by Pizarro when he entered the Inca kingdom were the emeralds, of immense size and worth. Some Spaniards broke the largest of the valuable gems, not knowing their worth. When the true nature of the Spaniard was discovered, many of the mines were hidden by the Indians. One emerald mine was rediscovered in

The Main Station as It Now Is

(293)

1815. Another lost mine supposed to be fabulously rich has just been rediscovered in Columbia. The search for it had gone on since the Indians buried it. Emeralds, carat for carat, are almost as valuable as diamonds. Mr. Stahl and his coworkers are finding in the Inca land, jewels of God more precious than emeralds or rubies or diamonds.

And still, in insistent, pleading voices, the calls are coming from the Quichua and Aymara Indians, Send us teachers; send us men who can lead us out of the bondage of drink and coca chewing, from the enslavement of filth and vice and superstition of the Egypt of the past, to the promised land of liberty and soberness and cleanliness and truth. Every call answered opens the doors of blessing, and more calls ensue. Thank God. Let the good work go on. May the Spirit of Him who said, "Go ye," rest in more and more abundant measure upon Pastor Stahl and his colaborers, and may the message of the gospel for this generation speedily reach the millions of Indians in "the Neglected Continent" who in the darkness of ignorance, superstition, and sin are longing for light and truth.

CHAPTER XIX

Among the Missions About Lake Titicaca

THE LAST WORD FROM MR. STAHL
(Review and Herald, January 8, 1920)

THE work is advancing rapidly in this mission these days. More than three hundred persons were baptized here during the first months of this year (1919). Many new calls are coming in, more than we can possibly answer this year.

At Pumata Station, where Brother and Sister Orley Ford have charge, the Sabbath attendance has increased so that the church building, large as it is, will have to be enlarged before the end of the year. These young people are earnest workers, and are having an excellent influence in their district.

The mission station is in a rather historic place. All around the station are the ancient Inca *chulpas,* or tombs. Not far from the mission home stands a gigantic mountain, Mount Liaquipa, towering to a height of 18,000 feet above sea level, and measuring nine miles around its base.

On the very summit are many houses built of stone. Even the roofs are of stone. En-

(295)

circling this mighty mountain are three immense stone walls thirty feet high, with openings in them at intervals. At each opening is the ruin of what at one time was a fine stone house. Evidently these were used by guards. These walls are about fifteen hundred feet apart, and are built on the very steepest part of the mountain. Everything about the mountain indicates that it was fortified to withstand some powerful enemy. Some say that at this place, some of the ancient Inca tribes made their last stand. Whatever it was, it is now the center of the work of a people seeking the living God.

Near the base of this mountain, we have a thriving mission, with four fine schools, and an average daily attendance of fifty children. Seventy-five persons were baptized at this place at the time of my last visit there, thus giving the church nearly three hundred members.

A few weeks ago Brother Ford and I paid a visit to Santiago Oji, a district that has been calling for a teacher for three years. This place is situated forty-five miles east of the Pumata Mission, on a peninsula inhabited by 20,000 Indians. As we neared the place, we

BAPTISM IN LAKE TITICACA

were met by Indians carrying flags, and the women showered us with flowers, to show their appreciation of our visit.

In the meetings that followed, great enthusiasm was manifested; and after a few days, forty came forward for baptism, even before a call had been made. We counseled them to wait, promising that some one would be sent as soon as possible to teach them more fully.

On our return, we stopped at Queñuani, the place where three years before the priests had stirred up hundreds of Indians to try to kill us, and where they so nearly succeeded. These two priests are now dead. One of these, when dying, sent for our missionary; and Brother Ford responded to the call, ministering to him in his last hours. The other, only a young man, died of a horrible contagious disease. Alone and without friends, he was buried by three Indians hired for the purpose.

These enemies are dead and forgotten, but the work of the Lord is advancing and prospering; and in this very place where they tried so hard to destroy and obliterate the work, there is a fine substation. We have

A ROAD ALONG THE EDGE OF A TWO THOUSAND FOOT PRECIPICE

there a school with fifty-nine pupils in daily attendance, the teacher, Raimondo Gomez, holding a session for the girls from 6 to 9 A. M., and for the boys from 9:30 A. M. to 2:30 P. M. Twenty-nine were baptized in Lake Titicaca on our last visit there. The lake was very rough at the time, but the people said they wanted to proceed with the ordinance. The waves were running so high that even before I could immerse the candidates, the waves had dashed over us; but the Indians took it all in good part, saying that the lake was rejoicing with them.

God has done some wonderful things for the people of this place, and in no other place in the whole field are the effects of the message seen as here. Men and women who seemed wholly given over to evil lives have turned to God. One woman especially is the wonder of the whole district. Three years ago she was wholly depraved, drunken and vicious, and feared by all. Her husband and children had driven her from her home, and she was utterly abandoned. She attended our first meetings in this district, and gave herself to God, and has ever since lived a most exemplary life. It was she who ran six miles to bring back our horses that had been cut loose and slashed at the time of the assault. She returned to her home and family; and as the result of the beautiful life she has since lived in Jesus, all her family have been baptized and are faithful members of the church. These words are frequently heard in this district: "If the gospel can do such things for people, then I want it also." I am glad that we have such a message, a *living* message.

After spending a few days with these people, Brother Ford and I separated, he to go home to his station, and I to go on to Puno, where the Lake Titicaca Indian Mission headquarters are now established. When I arrived, I found awaiting me a large delegation of Indians from the island of Imantana, who implored me to come and visit them. They had made two new boats of lake grass for our use, and had come so often that we simply could refuse them no longer; so I am making preparation to go with them.

Remember us at the throne of grace. The enemy is making every effort to destroy what we have done; so we must have help and wisdom from the dear Lord to go on with the work.

We invite you to view the complete
selection of titles we publish at:
www.TEACHServices.com

scan with your mobile
device to go directly
to our website

Please write or email us your praises, reactions, or
thoughts about this or any other book we publish at:

P.O. Box 954
Ringgold, GA 30736

Info@TEACHServices.com

TEACH Services, Inc., titles may be purchased in bulk
for educational, business, fund-raising, or sales
promotional use. For information, please e-mail:

BulkSales@TEACHServices.com

Finally if you are interested in seeing
your own book in print, please contact us at

publishing@TEACHServices.com

We would be happy to review your manuscript for free.

www.ingramcontent.com/pod-product-compliance
Lightning Source LLC
Chambersburg PA
CBHW071137160426
43196CB00011B/1920